Preface

You must never go down to the end of the town
if you don't go down with me.
A. A. Milne

There is nothing in this book which I have not used in practice, either by myself or with students. The aim is to provide the student with the tools for the job of investigating an urban environment at first hand—to find out, for example, how the town grew, and what sort of function it fulfils.

The methods outlined can be used separately or together, for large or small surveys, specialist or general, and may be put into practice at various levels of complexity. They can be a guide to developing personal techniques, and are therefore not only described but also discussed and their purpose considered.

In addition to method, there is some account—particularly towards the end—of principles and theory. Fieldwork which has pure description as its aim is not to be despised, but the activity is limited if it does not take theory into account. It should therefore be concerned with explanation and can often be used to test theory. For this reason I have endeavoured to stimulate thinking about the forces which produce the facts.

Geography is concerned not only with location but also with appearance. An attempt is therefore made in the book to venture into the field of townscape analysis; this is admittedly tentative and experimental but is included in the hope that it will encourage others to develop their own pioneer techniques.

Although the intention is to supply the tools rather than to set the tasks, some indication of what might be done is provided by a set of basic exercises at the end of the book. These are grouped to follow the order of the contents.

J. H.

y

ns

B.A.

LONDON: GEORGE PHILIP AND SON LIMITED

John Haddon, B.A., is Principal Lecturer in Geography and Head of Geography Department, Newton Park College, Bath. He is the author of *Local Geography: Geographical survey in rural areas* (George Philip, 1964) and *Discovering Towns* (Shire Publications, 1970).

Printed in Great Britain by
The Garden City Press Ltd., Letchworth,
Hertfordshire SG6 1JS

SBN 540 0021 9

Contents

Acknowledgement

Figures 1, 11, 20, 23, 24, 26 and 27 are based on Ordnance Survey maps and are printed with the permission of the Ordnance Survey

1. Scope and purpose

This book is concerned largely with how to collect facts—facts about the physical appearance of the town, about its economic functions, and about its pattern of growth—and it also deals with discovering relationships between the town and the country around. To make the fullest use of what we find, we must go further and consider what these facts mean in relation to the task of producing a good urban environment.

Towns are growing at an enormous rate, and the lives of the majority of people in our country are affected by the decisions of planners and developers, public authorities and private builders. If townspeople are ignorant of the details of their environment, if they have not given thought, on the basis of these facts, to the problems of that environment, they will be powerless to influence these planning decisions.

By studying our findings we can see the consequences of actions taken in the past, we can discover the forces that work to shape our town, and we can forecast the probable consequences of action taken now. Imagination and emotion are not enough—they must be informed by study. The imaginative idea must be submitted to the discipline of detailed expression in the light of known facts and must be tested against experience. To decide the way to go we must know where we are starting from. As Abraham Lincoln said, 'If we could first know where we are today, and whither we are tending, we could better judge what to do, and how to do it.'

We are talking about *geographical* surveys and therefore we are concerned with the town's physical appearance—with streets and buildings, parks and streams, hills and valleys, with the grouping of people, and with traffic. We want to find out where the factories are, where the shops, what kind they are and what they look like; where the houses are and where the flats; where the offices, cinemas, churches, and schools. And having located and described them, we need to find out why they are there and why they look the way they do; whether they are the right kind and in the right place. The mission is to seek, locate, describe, explain, and then to judge.

Any investigation must start with a question. This may be simply 'What is the distribution of x?', where x may be shops, or biscuit factories, or brick walls, or semi-detached houses. More fruitful questions are of the type 'What problems are posed by the pattern of distribution of x?', or 'How can the distribution of x be improved?'

The sort of questions we would be concerned with relate to the present state and possible alterations and additions to our town. Here is a mere handful out of the many possible ones:

1. Has the town a distinctive 'character'? Is this good or bad? Should new building preserve this character?
2. Is the present distribution of shopping facilities adequate? How should it be altered? Would it be best improved by providing some areas with better public transport to the town centre, or by developing regional centres?
3. Is industry located in places that spoil the amenities of the town? Is it located conveniently for transport, including the movement of people to work? Is the town in need of new or different industry? If so, where should it be put?
4. Are schools most conveniently located? Are the buildings of the best type? In view of changing concentrations of population, is there need for new schools, or the re-siting of old ones? (These questions could be asked about a whole range of services.)
5. Can the town be conveniently expanded? Should extension take place along the lines it has taken in the past, or should a change be made?
6. Is the present road system adequate for the traffic it carries? Where are the greatest volumes of traffic likely to be in the future? What is the best way of coping with these increased volumes?
7. Are the functions of the town mixed, or concentrated into separate areas? Is this good or bad? What should the future policy be?
8. Where are the present areas of buildings in poor condition? Should these buildings be replaced or renovated? What should be the future of the building or its site? Why have the buildings deteriorated? Can, or should, this be avoided in the future?
9. Should future house building be high-density or low-density? If both, how should the two types be distributed? Where are the most suitable and convenient places for house building?
10. Should the boundaries of the town be extended? If so, in what areas and for what purpose?

One question which investigators tend to fight shy of is the aesthetic one —is the thing beautiful? This should not be avoided, for the 'look' of a place or a building is part of its attributes and has an important influence. One of the advantages of geography is that it can make the student much more alive to his environment, he can see more, and life can become richer and more interesting for him. This increased awareness brings a greater sensitivity. No longer can it be said (with apologies to Wordsworth, himself no mean landscape geographer):

> A yellow warehouse by the river's brim,
> A yellow warehouse was to him,
> And nothing more.

The geographer may record that the warehouse was sited in relation to water transport of bulky goods and was today in the wrong place because the goods now come by road. He may note that its colour comes from the use of a particular local brick, and that its size and shape relates to the materials it is designed to store. The fact that it looks like a medieval castle he may attribute to Victorian romanticism. His survey is not, however, complete unless he adds that in his opinion it is a damnably ugly building, or alternatively, if this is what he thinks, that it is magnificently proportioned and very impressive. Indeed, the fact that there may be two opposing views should not deter him from making up his own mind, but it should make him consider his judgement carefully and endeavour to justify it. This means that he should endeavour to extend his experience by observing and reading as widely as possible.

Whatever section of the survey work you wish to develop, some further reading is advisable and books are therefore recommended in the appropriate places. Here, as a general introduction to ideas about urban geography, I want to suggest three works.

REFERENCES

Johns, Ewart, *British Townscapes*, Edward Arnold, 1965.

Johns himself writes that the book 'tries to explain an aspect of the appearance of towns as we find them today—that aspect which is the product of the impulse to design urban scenery'. He handles with great skill, and with admirable illustrations from drawings, photographs and maps, the variety of factors which go to make up the distinctive appearance of British towns, and although he does not deal with methods of study these are implicit in his handling of the data.

Jones, Emrys, *Towns and Cities*, Oxford Paperbacks University Series, 1966.

This is very much a world view, and a useful corrective to any narrowness which might result from a close attention to fieldwork in one town. It is full of both general ideas and detailed study, all presented in a pleasant style.

Smailes, A. E., *The Geography of Towns*, 5th edn. (rev.), Hutchinson University Library, 1966.

This paperback edition of a book first published in 1953 is worth acquiring for the broad general introduction it gives to the history and geography of towns in general. Its more detailed examples are taken from the British Isles. Due attention is paid to economic and social factors, but the study is firmly rooted in the geographical setting of the town and region.

2. Themes

How much to do?

The road to Hell, they say, is paved with good intentions, and the road to Town Study is littered with the wreckage of grand schemes of work abandoned in despair, and lightweight results so superficial as to be worthless. It is better to set yourself less than you think you can manage. In a small town, particularly with a team effort, it may be possible to cover all the main elements and produce a study of the whole. For a person working on his own, particularly in a large town, useful results are more likely to be obtained if he aims for one of the following:

(*a*) a detailed study of all the elements of a small area such as a suburb, a shopping centre, or a factory within the town.

(*b*) a set of sample studies; detailed studies of small areas chosen as representative of much larger regions within the town.

(*c*) a detailed study of one particular aspect of the whole town.

If very little time is available it would still be useful to make a study of one element in a small area, and there is a great deal to be said for doing a number of such little studies as practice in method before a bigger task is undertaken.

What to study?

A geographical study is concerned with cause and effect, the effects being the appearance of the place and the distribution of its elements. The appearance and distribution are geographical; the causes are not necessarily so.

The investigation can be approached from either end. We can map a distribution (garages, or bungalows, or grid-pattern streets, or brick buildings, or telephone kiosks, for example) and then try to find out why they are there. Or we can start with a factor, such as a railway line, a flood-plain, a coal mine, or a local inventor, and find out what effect it has had upon the geography of the town.

Argument arises here because some authorities would not consider it geographical to start with anything except a geographical factor, by which they usually mean a physical one. I would maintain, however, that anything which has a geographical *effect* is right for a geographer to study, and that just as when you study an effect you must consider non-geographical causes, so it is proper to begin with a non-geographical factor in order to arrive at a geographical result. These non-geographical factors are ideas; they are the minds of men. Just as it is appropriate and necessary in explaining the geography of Welwyn to examine the mind of Ebenezer Howard, so it would be proper to examine the mind first and then go on to discuss the place. It would therefore be reasonable to choose as topics 'The effect of the anti-slavery movement on the geography of Liverpool', 'Joseph Chamberlain as a factor in the geography of Birmingham', 'Civic pride and Leeds', 'Manchester and the Nonconformist conscience'.

Whether you start at one end with a *factor*, or at the other with a *feature*, will depend on your own interests and upon the nature of the town. You will decide this for yourself, but as a guide a few examples are given below.

FACTORS

Site—the whole site, or a particular element such as a river terrace, a flood plain, a steep slope, a plateau, a tributary valley, a particular outcrop of rock. This can be related to the whole town or to a particular aspect of it, such as street pattern, industry, or building materials.

Transport—such as the coming of the railway, the building of a motorway, the activities of a Turnpike Trust, the dredging of a river.

Economic resources—which are not necessarily those which exist today.

Outstanding local men—Bristol would not be the same without the Fry and Wills families, Stoke without the Wedgwoods, Newcastle without Grainger, Saltaire without Titus Salt, or Cowley without Morris.

Fashion—which rather unsatisfactory term covers a whole set of ideas about such things as architectural style, housing density, road layouts, and health.

Laws—the effect of some local law, such as an Improvement Act or an Enclosure Act, may have had a considerable effect on some aspect of town development, while the by-laws resulting from the various Health, Factory, and Planning Acts have had influence which sometimes dominates all other factors. Such laws are, of course, related to 'fashion' in politics and social philosophy.

Availability of land—this is affected by such things as the enclosure of a common, the sale of an estate, the extension of boundaries, improvements in drainage, earth-moving, and building techniques, and legal powers to obtain and destroy property. For example, the growth of Weston-super-Mare can be closely related to (*a*) enclosure of common land, (*b*) sale of Glebe (Church) land, (*c*) sale of three separate estates, (*d*) extension of Urban District boundaries, (*e*) improved methods of draining the marshes—and any one of these would make a small study in itself.

FEATURES

Street patterns—for example, these can be related to site, to fashion, to function, to barrier (old walls, railway lines, ownership boundaries, etc.), and to climate.

Building styles—relating to fashion, function, technology and site.

Functional zones—any one of which could be taken as a separate study, e.g. light industry, shopping, local administration offices, housing estates; even the siting of refuse dumps can in some cases make an interesting study.

Building materials—depending on availability, fashion, building technology, purpose, and price.

Townscape—the distinguishing of areas within the town by their characteristic building style and pattern.

Regional function—for example, administration, economic, social, educational.

3. Source material

Ordnance Survey

Maps for educational use can be bought at a discount from the Ordnance Survey, Romsey Road, Maybush, Southampton, or through the usual channels. When using an O.S. map, careful note should be made of the last date of revision; in many cases it will be necessary to bring the map up to date.

A brief summary of the most useful O.S. maps for town study is given below. It will be noticed that some information is given in the metric system. This is because of coming changes. The process of metrication will spread over many years and during that time maps with the old measurements will be circulating alongside those with the new, and some may even use both systems. A new levelling will give heights on bench mark lists in metres (to the nearest 0.01m), but for a time will also give feet. Contour intervals on the 1:25 000 and the new 1:10 000 will be 10m in regions of high relief, and 5m in low relief areas. The new 1:10 000 will replace the old 6-inch map.

All metric maps will be noticeably different in style, will carry the B.S.I. metric symbol or glyph and a prominent note, HEIGHTS IN METRES, and will have conversion scales. Eventually all heights will be metric, and this, apart from any new scales, is the main change. Present O.S. maps carry metric linear scales as well as imperial ones.

In geographical research it is advisable to use metric scales thoughout, but this will not always be possible and therefore references in this book are, where appropriate, given in both scales. Conversion tables are little help to learning, however; we need to 'think metric'.*

Ordnance Survey maps for town work

(*a*) 1:63 360 (1 inch to 1 mile): contours at 50ft intervals—spot heights. This is too small a scale to give more than a general idea of the town, but is useful for studying the regional setting. It will almost certainly be replaced by a 1:50 000 series which will use metric units.

(*b*) 1:25 000 ($2\frac{1}{2}$ inches to 1 mile; 4cm to 1km): contours at 25ft intervals (new edition, 5m in low relief, 10m in high)—spot heights. A very useful general map, particularly for the study of physical features.

* See Morris, J. A. 'Metrication in Geography', *Geography*, vol. 55, January 1970.

(*c*) 1:10 560 (6 inches to 1 mile): contours at 100ft intervals—spot heights—buildings to correct ground plan. This is probably the map you will use most unless you can afford the 1:2 500. It is to be superseded by the 1:10 000 (10cm to 1km) with contours at 5 or 10m intervals and spot heights in metres.

(*d*) 1:2 500 (25 inches to 1 mile; 40cm to 1km): no contours—spot heights—parcels of land numbered and areas given in acres (or, in future, in both acres and hectares). A very useful map.

(*e*) 1:1 250 (50 inches to 1 mile; 80cm to 1km): no contours—spot heights—house numbers—pavements shown. The most useful map for detailed survey, particularly if only a small area is being studied.

(*f*) 1:500 (126 inches to the mile). These town plans were produced between 1855 and 1894 and are out of print. They may, in some cases, be obtained from the Ordnance Survey, consulted in the British Museum, or found in the local library. They show great detail and are invaluable for reconstructing the geography of the Victorian town.

Early printed maps

Consult your town and country libraries about these. There may be a list such as Darlington and Howgego's *Printed Maps of London circa 1553–1850*, George Philip, 1964. The earliest map of your town is likely to be from John Speed's *Theatre of the Empire of Great Britain* (1612) or Camden's *Britannia* (1607 and later editions, including one of 1695 with maps by Norden).

After Speed there came an increasing number of town maps. Many of these relied heavily on Speed, and on other earlier maps, so that changes were often not incorporated until many years after they had taken place. Also some of the copies were not very accurate, and apparent changes in detail may simply be due to bad drawing. It may be possible to check this by reference to contemporary newspapers, guide books, rate books and directories.

Planning maps

Maps may have been made of particular changes such as the cutting of a road, railway or canal, the supply of water, or the provision of housing. These may be available at the Borough Council offices, the County offices, in the library, in the County Record office, or with the British Transport Historical Records, 66 Porchester Road, London W.2.

For post-war planning there will be a Town Map showing how the town is 'zoned' for development, and there will probably be other planning maps showing such features as land use, road development, and housing schemes. The Planning Authority will be either the Borough or the County.

In some cases the title deeds of buildings will have plans showing original siting. Details of town development may also be contained in Acts of Parliament and the library or Council offices will probably have copies.

Parish maps

Among the parish records there may be maps; if not, these may be lodged with the borough or county archives. The two most important—although a parish may have neither—are the Tithe Award and the Enclosure Award. The former followed the Tithe Commutation Act of 1836 and gives details of farmland and often of individual buildings; the latter, probably at some date between 1790 and 1840, gives details of common lands enclosed and apportioned by Act of Parliament.* Some, or all, of the agricultural and common land may now be covered by buildings.

There may also be Glebe Terriers, documents giving a detailed description of church lands and property.

Estate maps

Where part of a town was a private estate there may be old estate maps, either in the archives or in private hands. See Baker, 'Local history and early estate maps', *Amateur Historian*, Spring 1962. Baker suggests consulting the *Catalogue of Maps in the Essex Record Office 1566–1855*, which has a useful introduction to various types of maps and map-making.

Auctioneers' maps

Detailed maps of land to be sold by auction, sometimes showing the proposed building plots, are often useful for indicating what an area was like before it was developed and the way it was split up. The sale of estates is often closely connected with the development of town building.

OTHER SOURCES

Pictures

Prints and pictures can give a good deal of information about the townscape of the past and can help us to reconstruct the way the town has developed. Such illustrations may be found in local art galleries and in

* See Haddon, J., *Local Geography*, George Philip, 1964, pp. 31–32.

old books in the library. Sometimes prints can be bought quite cheaply in bookshops, especially if they are reproductions and not originals. It is a useful exercise to compare the old scene with the present one from the same viewpoints.

Useful detail can often be found in old photographs and postcards, and apart from local finds from private individuals, library or newspaper files, there may be relevant ones in the collection of the National Buildings Record, Fielder House, 10 Great College Street, London S.W.1, or in the Prints and Drawings section of the British Museum.

Finally, it may be helpful to consult air photographs. The Borough Council may have had some taken, or you may be able to get them from the Air Ministry or from a private firm such as Aerofilms Ltd., 4 Albemarle Street, London W.1.

Newspapers

In addition to photographs, the local paper will carry reports about changes in the town such as new buildings, boundary alterations, destruction by fire, and new transport arrangements. Files of newspapers may be found in the town library, in some cases conveniently on microfilm, or they may be consulted—although not invariably—at the newspaper offices. Considerable self-discipline is needed to prevent the time-consuming distraction of reading a vast amount of fascinating but irrelevant matter; fortunately, newspaper layouts remain fairly constant and you soon get to know exactly where to look for the type of information you are seeking. The correspondence columns should not be neglected, nor the advertisements which are often a useful guide to the business activities of the town.

Directories

These, including telephone directories, are useful for locating businesses (*see figure 1*) and industries at different periods in the town's history, and also for tracing the time when new streets were made.

Rate Books

Such books, both Corporation and Parish, are the precursors of the modern Rating Registers which can be consulted by arrangement with the Borough Rating Officer.* The old Rate Books, if they still exist, may

* See Davies, Giggs and Herbert, 'Directories, rate books and the commercial structure of towns', *Geography*, vol. 53, January 1968. Among other matters, the authors describe the use of a Rate Index found by dividing gross rateable value by ground-floor area.

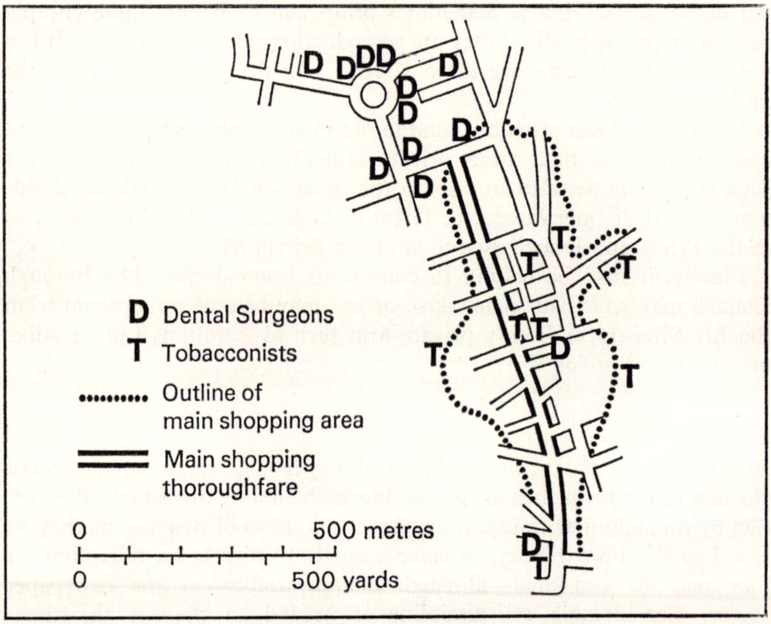

Figure 1 Distribution of dentists and tobacconists in central Bath

Based on the Classified Telephone Directory, 1963. This map brings out an interesting contrast in location, but it must be noted that:

(*a*) Probably more dentists than tobacconists have telephones; the list of dentists therefore is more likely to be complete.

(*b*) On the other hand, some dentists share telephones.

(*c*) A field-check showed only two extra tobacconists and no extra locations for dentists but a considerable sharing of premises. This is not sufficient to invalidate any conclusions we may come to about location on the basis of the telephone directory.

be held by the Parish, the Borough Council, the local library, or the County archivist. The books usually record rateable values and/or rates paid, and although they do not usually identify individual buildings they are useful in showing how values and occupancy altered. With modern lists the buildings can be identified.

Corporate property

The Corporation will probably own property in the town, including council housing estates. Information can be obtained from the Housing Manager, the Corporate Property Surveyor, and the Medical Officer of Health. Deeds of such property will be with the Town Clerk's Legal Department.

Council minutes

The Borough or Urban District Council's actions can have a considerable effect on the geographical development of a town. Their minutes are now usually published monthly and may be obtained most conveniently from the town library, which may also hold older reports.

Commissioners' minutes

Nineteenth- and late eighteenth-century development was usually in the hands of Improvement Commissioners appointed by an Act of Parliament, and if their minute books and accounts are available they should be consulted if you are studying the growth of the town or some particular aspect of it. A variant of the Commissioner idea was used when the New Towns Act of 1950 made provision for a Development Corporation to be set up to plan and build each New Town.

Service undertakings

A town provides a wide variety of services for its inhabitants. These are of geographical importance because they give rise to townscape features and also have had an influence on the growth of the town. Often the various bodies have maps and plans of their undertakings. Such service installations include Gas, Electricity, Water, Sewerage, Transport, Education, Recreation, and Hospitals. Usually these services were first provided by private enterprise before being taken over by public bodies.

Local histories

Look these up in the library, but be wary, they vary a great deal in reliability and should be checked as far as possible with other sources. On the other hand there is no need to repeat a lot of research which has already been done by a reliable authority.

Published statistics

A useful summary is the Index to Sources given in an appendix to the *Annual Abstract of Statistics* published by H.M.S.O. and available in large libraries. (Another useful appendix gives the minimum Standard Industrial Classification.) The *Abstract* itself is on a national basis and is therefore only useful in local study for comparing your town with the nation as a whole.

Another source is the decennial Census of Population, started in 1801. Less frequent are the Censuses of Production and of Distribution. It should be noted, however, that a Census is out-of-date by the time it is published, and that the area for which figures are given is too large for the purposes of local study. A Municipal Borough will be listed separately, but other towns will be included with Urban and Rural Districts; and the total figures for a Borough, even when given for Wards, are a poor guide to the considerable diversity within the area. It is possible, however, that the Local Authority has collected statistics for planning purposes and an application to the Town Clerk may enable you to see these.

A note on using the library

It follows from the above accounts of sources that whatever theme you choose to investigate you will need to spend some time in libraries. After you have familiarised yourself with your town by studying maps and walking round it, you should visit the library. The lending department will have books on local history and geography which you may borrow, but most of what you want will be in the reference department. You should familiarise yourself with their index system. This is normally a card index arranged under authors and subjects. You can start by looking in the subject index under the name of your town and then proceed to the various topics; for example an Improvement Act might be found under 'I' for improvement, 'A' for Act, or 'P' for Parliament. In some cases there may be a special index for local history. Make a note of the various references with the title, author, and library reference number. Ask the assistant for the book or document you want, or hand in the slip which many libraries provide. The book will not necessarily be on the shelves.

Material with Borough or County Archivists may not be catalogued, but if there is a catalogue or hand list it should be consulted if possible. It is best to get in touch with the archivist by letter, explaining exactly what sort of material you want to see and saying when you can come.

When visiting libraries and record offices, go prepared with notebook, pen, tracing paper, pencil, etc. for taking notes. You may be allowed to photograph documents, or there may very likely be facilities for providing you with photostat copies at a small fee.

REFERENCES

Ashworth, W., *The Genesis of Modern British Town Planning*, Routledge & Kegan Paul, 1965.

This very readable and interesting book takes us through the social, economic and political forces behind the nineteenth-century development of British towns and carries on with town planning up to 1947. In addition it is a guide to sources and has a very useful bibliography.

Clayton, R. (ed.), *The Geography of Greater London*, G. Philip, 1964.

This excellent book, with a very full bibliography, serves two purposes.

It sets an example for urban study by a series of chapters on London, and it gives details of methods of study to be used. These study methods are related to work in schools but are easily adapted to more advanced work, and although the examples are taken from London the techniques can be applied to any town.

Hoskins, W. G., *Local History in England*, Longman, 1959.

Anyone interested in local study, whatever branch, should read this book. There are two chapters on towns, but there is much else in the rest of the book which is of use in urban study.

Jackson, J. N., *Surveys for Town and Country Planning*, Hutchinson University Library, 1963.

This is a basic text for methods of urban survey, dealing with both sources and method. Written with clarity and economy of style, it covers a great deal of ground in a soundly practical manner.

4. Recording methods

The object of fieldwork is to collect information in such a way that it can be processed and studied. The information must therefore be as complete as is needed for its use, it must be clear, and it should preferably be cast in some standard form. Part of it will be collected as sketches and photographs, part as maps, part as answers to questions, but mostly as records of observations in the field. We will deal with the last of these first.

Recording on field sheets

There must be an exact statement of the location in the field of the object recorded and this usually means reference to a map. In towns the best scale for this is 1 : 1 250, but as each sheet covers only a small area it is more likely that you will be using the 1 : 2 500 series. It is possible to use the 1 : 10 560 but it is difficult to mark in individual detail.

The basic reference map which you carry in the field should be marked so that every object you record has a reference number. Thus every building, street, open space, and so on, for which you intend to make an observation should be given a reference number on the map. This number should be in waterproof ink and clearly legible; red ink is more clearly distinguishable.

To avoid the need for long numbers you can start afresh with each metre square of the National Grid. Thus 7263/46 would refer to a building in square 7263, while 7264/46 would refer to one in the next square to the east. Putting on numbers is a fiddling business and is best done before you go out, although more may have to be added in the field. Other corrections will probably have to be made to show changes since the map was last revised, and it is best to do this on a preliminary reconnaissance.

For simple surveys when, for example, only one element—such as land use at ground level, or distribution of building material—is being recorded, the information can be entered directly on the map and no reference numbers will be needed. In such cases it is also possible to record on sketch maps drawn in the field, the information being transferred afterwards. The sketch map can consist of a double line up the centre of the page to represent the street, with information entered to left and right.

With more complicated information you will need a recording sheet ruled so that entries can be made in an orderly manner. These entries will have to be in code or they will take up too much room. Examples of recording sheets and codes are given later in the book.

Maps and recording sheets should be clipped to hardboard, and, in designing the sheet, space should be left at the top where the clip will come. Instead of a clip a rubber band may be used and in windy weather it is advisable to have a second clip or band to keep the paper from blowing about. In showery weather it is helpful to have a waterproof cover such as a plastic bag.

As a recording sheet is normally used in conjunction with a map, it is useful to have a second board. This can be hinged to the first with tape so that map and sheet can be seen side by side. Alternatively the map can be fixed to the back of the recording board. Entries should be neat and unambiguous, and made with a fine ball-point or well-sharpened pencil; this can be attached to the board by a string. It is useful to have a pocket notebook for recording extra information. The type which is bound at the top with a wire spiral is convenient.

Designing a recording sheet

Basically, a recording sheet consists of a set of vertical columns crossed by a set of horizontal rows, forming a grid. The columns represent the objects being surveyed and the rows the characteristics of each object, or vice versa. Thus, if you wanted to make a survey of the ground-floor of every building in a certain area, you might allocate each row to a building and have one column only in which you entered use:

Building	Ground-floor
West St. 1.	Grocer's shop
2.	Dwelling
3.	

Figure 2

To save space and time you could devise a code for land use and simply insert the appropriate code-number after each building. An even simpler way, which has the advantage of forming a visual pattern, would be to have a number of columns, one for each type of land use, and put a tick in the appropriate column after each building, as shown overleaf.

Building	R	S	F	W	O	P	
West St. 1.		✓					
2.	✓						
3.							

Figure 3

R = residence; S = shop; F = factory; W = warehouse; O = office; P = public building

If, however, you want to note more than one thing about each building it would be time-wasting to keep on visiting it, recording one thing at a time. In this case the recording will have to contain a labelled column for each type of thing recorded. If, for example, you wanted to know the ages of the buildings, the materials of which their walls were constructed, their roofing materials, and their state of repair, the sheet could be ruled like this:

Building	Age	Walls	Roof	Repair
West St. 1.	19	B	Sl	G
2.	18	S	T	P
3.				

Figure 4

Age = by centuries; *Materials:* S = stone, B = brick, C = concrete, W = wood, Sl = slate, T = tile, O = other; *State of repair:* E = excellent, G = good, P = poor.

Once again a code is needed since there is not room to write out the entries in full. It may still be possible to split the columns and make entries by ticking, but the more things you want to record the more difficult it is to find enough room. Where there are a lot of features to record it may be more convenient to use the rows for them.

In constructing the sheet make sure that you leave enough room for headings and for each entry. Rule up a sheet in pencil and use it in the field before deciding on the final form.

Photography and field sketching

Most town survey recording is expressed in maps but these leave out a very important part of the townscape—the vertical surfaces of buildings. In order to show building faces you will need to use photographs and/or sketches. Good drawings are often more useful than photographs as they cut out irrelevant detail and can cover a greater extension in width and height.

Photographs and sketches are needed to illustrate certain main classes of things:

(*a*) a building typical of an area or street, of particular importance due to its style and/or function, or anomalous (i.e. distinctively unlike the type normal for the area);
(*b*) panoramas, or whole streets;
(*c*) views to show effect of grouping;
(*d*) detail of structure or ornament.

In all cases the picture when presented must be clearly labelled to show its identity. The time, date and weather conditions should be given, the place from which the photograph or sketch was made, and the particular points which it illustrates.

Photography

Although there are times when you will want to show the whole street clutter, your main difficulty will be to get a clear, uninterrupted view of the building or buildings. For such views Sundays or early morning, when traffic is least, are best. A wide-angle lens is particularly useful for photographing buildings and street scenes, while a telephoto lens will help with details and also for photographing whole buildings from a distance. A certain amount of side-lighting is necessary to bring out surface modelling and daylight flash can help with this. A light meter is almost essential.

Rather than carry a straggle of straps round your neck it is better to have a large satchel; this can carry not only photographic equipment but also your maps, notebooks, pencils, and other paraphernalia, including sandwiches (providing they are well-wrapped).

Sketching

The chief problems here are proportion and perspective. With regard to proportion, for all practical purposes we can eliminate the problem for individual frontages by measurement. This can be done by looking with one eye past a ruler held at arm's length and transferring the measurements onto squared paper, using a suitable scale. For my own purposes I have found that measurements given by a ruler held at a comfortable arm-stretch transfer to a sheet of paper squared in milli-

Figure 5 An annotated sketch of a Georgian terrace, Albemarle Road, Clifton, Bristol. Built in 1762.

metres at a scale of one centimetre to five millimetres, but obviously this varies with the length of your arm, the size of the building, and your distance from it. True scale can be determined by measuring the actual frontage of the building and scaling it down to the width of the drawing.

It is not necessary to measure all the distances; once a few basic proportions are established the rest can be related by eye. Considerable errors can be introduced if the ruler is not always held at the same distance from the eye and if the observer does not stay in the same place. Some people find it useful to fasten the ruler (or perhaps a squared grid on transparent material such as Perspex) to a cord which can be held in the teeth.

If you work from an easel, a simple sighting attachment could be added to it. For the actual drawing, if it is to be detailed, you will need a hard, well-sharpened pencil, or a fine ball-point, or pen and ink. For broader effects, a soft pencil, a broader ball-point or a felt-tipped pen are suitable. Drawings should be clearly titled and dated, and some measurements given, such as the width of a building. These field sketches can be re-drawn, preferably with pen and Indian ink and with the help of a ruler, but you must be careful that in doing this you do not make improvements that are really falsifications.

Perspective would not be a problem if we could draw things as we actually see them. Unfortunately we know from experience the shapes and sizes of the things we see and therefore we tend to draw them as they are, rather than how they look; in particular we are blind to the small variations in slope which make a line drawing look solid. It is therefore necessary to train ourselves by studying the rules of perspective. This is too large a subject to deal with here but help can be got from books such as *Drawing Perspective* by H. Chevins and *Buildings* by R. Downer (both in the Studio Vista Drawing Books series), and *Perspective* by V. Perard, No. 22 of the Pitman Art Books.

Panorama sketches are one useful means of adding an extra dimension to the information given on maps. They were popular in the eighteenth century and can give useful information about that period. It is probably best to simplify an old print by tracing the outlines of the principal buildings and physical features—in some cases it need be only the skyline. If this sketch is then taken to the place from which it was originally drawn, it may be possible to indicate changes by drawing them in a different colour. Unfortunately the view may have been blocked by subsequent building, and in this case you must look for a point in a nearby position, or find a useful roof, and make an adjustment for the change of position.

Even if you have not got an old drawing for comparison, a simple panoramic sketch from a well-chosen viewpoint will make a useful illustration. Detailed instruction is given in *Landscape Drawing* by G. E. Hutchings (Methuen); the beginner should not be put off by the expertise shown in the illustrations—simple outlines without shading can be very effective, particularly for buildings.

A panorama can also be built up from a series of photographs providing there is a slight overlap and that the camera is kept at the same level, preferably by using a tripod. Your choice of viewpoint will probably be limited by the nature of the ground, but you should try to find one from which you can illustrate some particular feature, such as the relationship between building and relief, or the concentration of certain types of activity.

Plans

Plans of individual buildings can be used to show the use to which particular rooms are put and to give details of frequently recurring types of buildings. They can also be used to show how the outward form of a building is related to its function and the construction methods used.

A further relationship of some importance is between building and the law, particularly since the Public Health Act of 1875 and subsequent Acts and by-laws made under them which laid down minimum requirements in respect of such features as lighting, room-size, building materials, street width, and sanitation. Nineteenth-century 'by-law building' tended to be extremely monotonous as the minimum requirements became, for the sake of economy, the maximum, and—as is often still the case—much design was controlled by the need or desire to build as cheaply as possible without infringing the regulations.

Measuring for plans is usually done with 50ft (15m) linen and 6ft (2m) steel tapes but it is useful to have a folding wooden rule as well, particularly if there is no one to hold the other end of the tape. The usual scale for drawing has been 1ft to ⅛th of an inch, but it is more convenient to work on squared paper to a scale of 1ft to 1/10th inch (or 1m to 1cm). If squared paper is carried a plan can be drawn quickly on the spot which will reveal any mistakes or inadequacies in your measuring.

Briefly, the procedure is to draw an unmeasured rough plan, enter the measurements on it, and from these draw a scale plan on squared paper. It is important to measure the thickness of all walls. Door, window, fireplace, and cupboard measurements should be of the openings, ignoring surrounds. Note which way the doors open and on which side they are hinged. If the room is not rectangular, diagonals should be measured—they are in any case a useful check. Heights of rooms and other details such as type of flooring, windows (e.g. sash or casement), doors, use of room, presence of electricity, etc. should be noted. Clues to the building history come from changes in wall thickness (for example, an old outside wall may have become a thick interior dividing one when the house was enlarged), floor level, building material, and roof lines.

Transects

The techniques which have been mentioned can often be usefully employed along a line through the town, or part of the town. This is a transect ('cross cut') and is a useful way of obtaining a quick look at the way a town has grown. It is dealt with in more detail on pages 119-20.

5. Statistical analysis

We cannot do more in the space available than indicate one or two ways in which statistics can be used, and to introduce some of the more common terms. For a proper understanding of the subject, reference should be made to books on statistics and in particular to:

Chorley, R. J. and P. Haggett (eds.), *Frontiers in Geographical Teaching* (Chapter XII), Methuen, 1965.

Cole, J. P. and C. A. M. King, *Quantitative Geography*, Wiley, 1968.

Gregory, S., *Statistical Methods and the Geographer*, Longman, 1963.

Loveday, R., *Statistics*, 2nd edn. (rev.), Cambridge University Press, 1970.

Monkhouse, F. J. and H. R. Wilkinson, *Maps and Diagrams* (Appendix), 2nd edn., Methuen, 1964.

Theakstone, W. and C. Harrison, *The Analysis of Geographical Data*, Heinemann, 1970.

Quantification

Some of the information we collect can be expressed in number. Examples are areas; lengths; counts of various things such as people, traffic, number of shops; ranks (things placed in order according to a characteristic such as size); and proportions (e.g. percentages). These are quantitative (as opposed to qualitative) expressions, and have certain advantages:

(*a*) They are less subjective; that is, they depend less upon the feelings or opinions of the observer. This is not to say they are unaffected by the observer; there is always an element of experimental error, and in any case the decision of what to measure and how to measure it is partly subjective.

(*b*) They lend themselves more easily to comparison. Here again there are limitations to their use as they are comparisons of quantity only.

(*c*) They enable us to make precise statements. We must, however, be careful, for we may easily imagine that we are being more exact than we really can be. There are limits to precision, depending upon our methods of measurement, and there are other limits set by the way in which we treat the information. There is a great danger of misunderstanding if statistics are handled by people who do not understand on what basis they have been collected and the limitations of the manipulations carried out afterwards. As J. N. Jackson writes,

'It is sound advice to be suspicious, rather than to accept statistics at their face value . . . He (the planner) must either be able to interpret the data competently himself, or be aware of this deficiency and be willing to rely on appropriate advice.'*

(*d*) They can be presented in a variety of ways which are visually effective—charts, maps, diagrams, graphs, equations, etc.

(*e*) By manipulation they can often tell us something about relationships. It is this which makes up the bulk of much geographical analysis, and is concerned with explanation in geography. We take up one or two aspects of the study of relationships below.

Distribution of points

We are often concerned with the distribution of a single phenomenon, such as towns of a certain size, or a certain type of factory. Statistically all the things of a class (e.g. all men, all Chinese, all pillar boxes) form a *universe*; those within an area being studied are called a *population*; and a single member is an *individual*.

As geographers we are concerned to find out what causes the population to be distributed in a particular way. Before pursuing our enquiries, it would be as well to know whether the distribution could have arisen by mere chance, that is, whether it is *random*. The two extremes are an *aggregated* distribution where the whole population is clumped together, and a *uniform* one where it is evenly distributed over the whole area. In between there are various degrees of randomness.

Of several techniques for studying distribution the *nearest-neighbour analysis* is a useful one. In this we measure the straight-line distance from each point to its nearest neighbour and average the results arithmetically. This observed mean distance is called $\bar{r}_0$. The expected mean distance, $\bar{r}_E$, in a random distribution is $\frac{1}{2}p^{-\frac{1}{2}}$ where p is the density of points per unit area (e.g. if the distances are measured in metres then p is the total area in square metres divided by the total number of points). The nearest-neighbour measure (R) is found by dividing $\bar{r}_0$ by $\bar{r}_E$, using the formula:

$$R = 2\bar{d}\sqrt{\frac{n}{A}}$$

where: $\bar{d} = \bar{r}_0$ A = area concerned n = number of points

If R is 1 the distribution is random, if 0 it has maximum aggregation, and if 2.15 it is an even distribution. These three cases can be pretty well determined by eye; what is important is that for the in-between cases the

* *Surveys for Town and Country Planning*, Hutchinson University Library, 1963.

analysis gives us a measure of the degree of aggregation, randomness, or uniformity, and this is particularly useful when distributions in different areas are being compared.

Relationship of variables

In studying the facts of geography we are studying things which are in the process of change—that is, there is a variation over time; an obvious example is the change of population in a town over the years. The facts of geography not only change in time but also in space; in a town it can be observed that the number and type of shops, the heights of buildings, the amount of traffic, for example, vary between different areas in the town. We may then want to know if there is any regular connection we can find and state between changes in time and changes in geography, or changes in location and changes in geography. For example, is the rate of change of population the same over time, and if it varies, does it vary in some way which can be expressed mathematically? In space, does the density of housing vary according to distance from the town centre, and if so does it do so in any regular way? And if something varies in time or space according to a definable pattern, are there other things which vary to the same pattern which would indicate, though not prove, that there is some probability of one causing the other? (We must be careful—that changes in one thing occur at the same time as changes in another does not necessarily mean that one change is causing the other.)

Changes are usually expressed as graphs where one thing is plotted against another, particularly against time or distance. It is extremely unlikely that the observed figures will produce a smooth graph; the points will probably be scattered. The first job is therefore to produce a *best-fit* graph. This is usually done by drawing a *regression curve* on the principle of *least squares*, that is, by drawing a curve (which may be a straight line) in which the sum of the squares of the distances of the points from the curve is at a minimum (there are *two* such curves, according to whether you regress on x or on y).

A normal straight-line curve represents a development in a series of equal steps. If however the population increases at a greater and greater amount the line will be curved; where the population increases in geometrical progression the curve has a form which is known as *exponential*, increasing more and more rapidly in slope. Such a set of figures can, however, be made to produce a straight line if the logarithms are plotted instead of the actual figures; this is facilitated by the use of log-linear graph paper on which the figures can be entered directly without first calculating the logarithms.

One value of the regression line is that we can calculate the extent to which individual observed values deviate from it, and therefore the extent to which the curve can be considered a reliable representation of the data. If the best-fit curve approximates reasonably well to the observed figures it may then be possible to express as an equation the relationship which produces a graph of this type. A straight-line graph is given by the formula $Y = a + bX$, where a and b are numbers which remain constant and are known as *parameters*. The least-squares calculation will give these parameters and the formula can be used as a description of the relationship between X and Y.

Classifying the population

It may not be appropriate to assume that every individual in the population is equal. For example, if we make a count of butcher's shops we may be including very small and very large ones, and the fact that one area has 12 and another 2 may be a very poor indication of the importance of the shops in each area if the 12 are very small and the 2 are very large. Similarly, a simple count of 20 vehicles passing a point might be of 20 bicycles, 20 lorries, or a mixture of various types. We may therefore need to devise a standard unit and express each individual in terms of multiples or fractions of that unit. We might, for example, not count a shop as 1, but give it a number equal to the number of people it employs, or its annual sales turnover, or the length of its frontage.

Sometimes proportions are more important than quantities. It may be more meaningful to know that 25% of all workers in a town, or in a certain area in the town, are employed in cotton mills than to know that there are 300 of them. And if we want to know whether the 25% is an unusual proportion we can compare it with the national average for all towns.

In other cases we may need to weight our individual observations by multiplying them by some number. An example of this is the T/E index given on page 102, but this weighting is done to produce a more accurate figure whereas weighting is usually for the purpose of emphasising the importance of some particular feature. If for example we were studying the location of small shopping centres, we might well consider what sort of shops people needed near at hand. Some shops we might judge more important than others—a grocer we might consider more important for daily needs than a shoe shop. If then we count a shoe shop as 1 we may decide to count a grocer as 4, and perhaps a tobacconist as 3. So a street with a shoe shop and a tobacconist would rate as 4, which is the same as a street with only a grocer in it. The weighting this illustrates is very crude; a better one would have to be based on the actual shopping preferences as expressed in a questionnaire.

Ranking

Comparisons are important. The simplest ones are where we just note that one area has more of something than another area. Thus we may divide up our town and then count (either crudely or in terms of a standard index) the number of, say, schools in each area. We can then arrange, or rank, the areas according to the number they contain.

If we do this for a number of different things we may find that certain areas keep on coming out with the same rank number—the gasworks region might keep on coming out bottom (except for gas). The extent of *rank correlation* will depend on the kinds of things we are counting—we would expect that we would get much the same sort of order for shops and offices but not for shops and factories.

To find out how similar the rankings are, we can use a rank correlation index. The most usual is Spearman's which compares the ranking of two sets of things. If, for example, area 'A' is ranked 1 for one thing and 4 for another we take the difference between the two ranks (3) and square it (9). We do this for all the areas and add the results. We then multiply this by 6, divide the result by the cube of the number of areas minus the number of areas, and take the final result away from one. It is expressed more neatly by the formula:

$$R = 1 - \frac{6\Sigma d^2}{n^3 - n}$$

where:

R = rank correlation coefficient (sometimes given as p, 'rho')
Σ = the sum of all the values of the variable following this symbol
d = difference in rank position
n = number of terms in the rank list

The limits are +1 (perfect, positive correlation) and −1 (perfect, negative correlation, where the ranking is reversed in the second set).

If we get a figure between +1 and −1 we need to know if this could be the result of chance. To find out we have to apply another test. Such a test is *Student's t*, where t equals R multiplied by the square root of two less than the number of pairs, the result divided by the square root of 1 minus R squared, that is:

$$t = \frac{R\sqrt{n-2}}{\sqrt{1-R^2}}$$

where:

t = *Student's t* R = rank correlation coefficient
n = number of pairs (which must not be less than 10)

To see how far this figure is significant we look it up on a *Student's t* graph in a set of statistical tables. The degree of significance is the extent to which two things may occur together by chance, and the graph will give us *t* figures which indicate 0.1%, 1%, 5%, and 10% chances that the correlation is significant—i.e. the 5% figure indicates that there is only a chance of five times in a hundred that the relationship between the two sets of rankings could occur by chance. To use the table we also need to know how many areas we have observed, for the more we have used the lower is the value of *t* which will give us a required degree of significance. It is not however the total number we use in consulting the table, but the number of *degrees of freedom*. If we have a list of 10 things, then when we have arranged 9 in order we have no freedom of choice in placing the last one so the degrees of freedom are 9; if there are *n* places there will be $n-1$ degrees of freedom. In comparing pairs, as we are doing in rank correlation, it is the final *pair* which have no freedom and the degree of freedom is $n-2$.

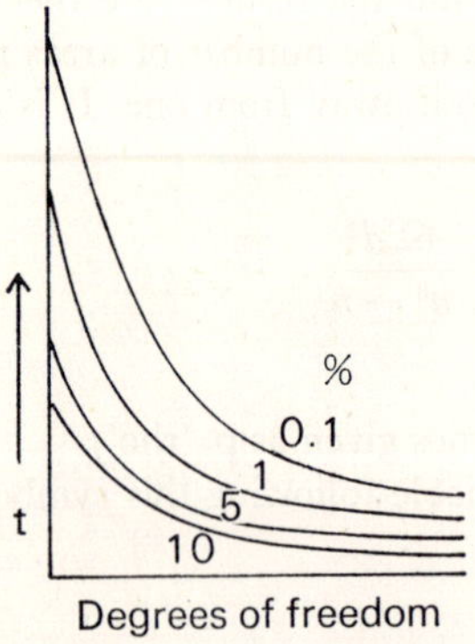

Figure 6 Layout of 'Student's t' graph

This is not the only, nor indeed the chief use of *Student's t*, which is applied mainly to the significance of variations between small samples in the form of

$$\frac{\text{Error in sample mean}}{\text{Standard error of mean of whole population}}$$

Variation in density

If we want to find out if there is a statistically significant relationship between the distribution of a population and the areas in which it is located, that is, the frequency with which individuals occur in each of the areas, we can apply the *chi-square* (χ^2) test (chi is pronounced 'ki'). For this we need not only an observed frequency (*O*) but also an expected frequency (E). E may be an even distribution or it may be based on some hypothesis of how the population is likely to be distributed.

The chi-square figure is obtained by subtracting for each area the estimated from the observed frequency, squaring the result, dividing it by the estimated frequency, and adding together the results for all the areas. It can therefore be expressed as

$$\chi^2 = \sum \frac{(O - E)^2}{E}$$

where:

χ^2 = frequency distribution

O = observed frequency

E = expected or theoretical frequency

The figure is then checked against a graph or tables, using the appropriate degrees of freedom and the appropriate percentage level.

Note that we are concerned with *frequencies,* i.e. the number of occurrences, not with measures, such as length or area. We would, for example, count the number of shops, not measure the area they occupy, for chi-squared would work out differently according to whether we took square feet or square metres. Things counted could be physical objects such as empty houses or road intersections, events such as the number of road accidents in a year, or relationships such as the number of times two features appear together.*

An example might investigate geology and industry. Suppose that there are three major rock types—alluvium, clay, and sandstone. Calculate the percentage of the total area which is occupied by each. Count the number of industrial establishments (divided, if necessary, into a number of classes) on each formation. Calculate an expected frequency by allocating a percentage of the total number of establishments to each formation according to the percentage of land occupied by that formation; for example, if 50% of the land is clay, the expected frequency of factories will be 50% of the whole. This assumes that geology has no effect on the number of factories and is therefore a *null hypothesis.* Now apply the chi-square test to see if the null hypothesis is valid or not. If as a result the null hypothesis can be rejected, we have grounds for continuing to look for a connection between geology and industry.

* See Teaching Geography No. 11, The Geographical Association, 1970.

Variations from a mean

Suppose we have a list of measurements of the same thing taken either for different areas at the same time or for the same area for different times; this might be the rainfall on a particular day for twelve places in the town, or it might be the daily rainfall for one station for a year. What one figure can we give to indicate the general, or average, condition?

We may take the *mode,* which is the one that occurs most frequently; the *median* which is the figure for the middle entry when the numbers are arranged in order of size; or the *arithmetic mean,* which is the sum of the quantities divided by the total number of entries on the list. There are also the *geometric* and *harmonic* means which need not concern us here. For statistical purposes the arithmetic mean is most commonly used, but in a short list it can be seriously affected by one very large or one very small quantity and this can make it a very poor indicator.

Having established a mean we need some way of expressing how far individual figures deviate from it. We can do this by taking each figure away from the mean, adding the results (ignoring whether the sign is + or −), and dividing by the total number of entries in the list. This gives us the *mean deviation.* If we add the squares of the differences and divide by the number of entries, we have the *variance,* and if we take the square root of the variance we have the *standard deviation,* which is written s or σ (sigma).

$$\sigma = \sqrt{\frac{\Sigma (x - \bar{x})^2}{n}}$$

where:

σ = standard deviation of the whole population
x = an individual value
$\bar{x}$ = the average value of all the x's
n = number of terms

σ is used to indicate the standard deviation within a whole population, and s for the standard deviation obtained from samples, the more usual case. For some purposes we have to use a *best estimate,* which is indicated by putting a circumflex over the symbol—$\hat{\sigma}$.
The best estimate is found from the equation

$$\hat{\sigma} = s\sqrt{\frac{n}{n - 1}}$$

where:

$\hat{\sigma}$ = the best estimate of the standard deviation of the whole population
s = the standard deviation of the sample
n = number of terms in the sample

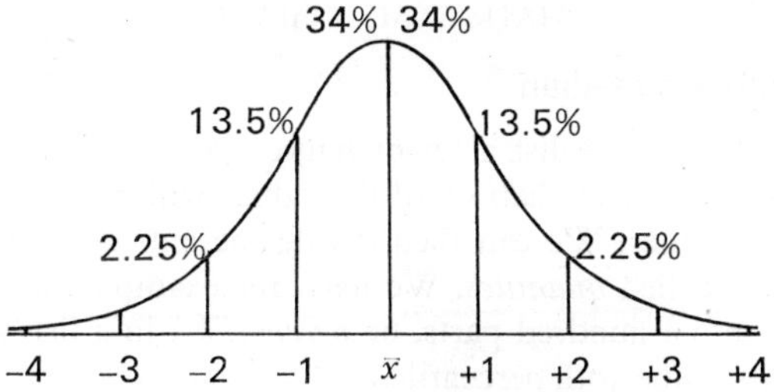

Figure 7 Percentage of occurrences in a normal distribution curve

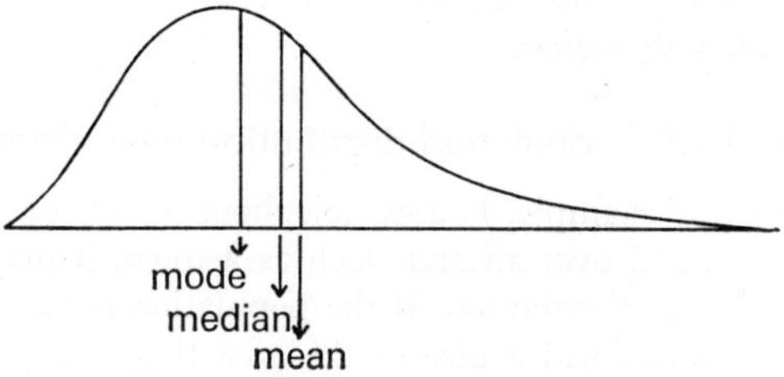

Figure 8 A skewed distribution. This is a positive skew; if it 'tailed' the other way it would be negative.

For the many and varied uses of these parameters a textbook on statistics must be consulted, but it may be mentioned here that one of the virtues of the standard deviation is that in a normal distribution curve, which is symmetrical about the mean ($\bar{x}$), 68.3 % of the occurrences will fall between $+ 1\sigma$ and -1σ of the mean, and 95.45 % will fall between $+ 2\sigma$ and -2σ. If, however, the distribution is not normal but is skewed, that is, the mean lies to one side of the median so that the curve is not symmetrical, our prediction, still using the standard deviation, might be related to another standard curve known as a Poisson distribution. Generally speaking, normal distribution applies to continuously varying phenomena, such as slope, and Poisson to individual, discrete, phenomena.*

To compare two distribution curves we can calculate for each curve its *coefficient of variation*, which is the percentage of $\bar{x}$ formed by σ, that is,

$$\frac{\sigma}{\bar{x}} \times 100.$$

* See Gregory, S., *Statistical Methods and the Geographer*, Longman, 1963, pp. 75–81.

Deviation from the median

We have seen that if we list a set of figures in order of magnitude, the middle one is the median; half of all the values will be on one side of this and half on the other. We can then divide the entries on each side into equal quantities called *quantiles*. We may, for example, divide the whole list of entries into a hundred parts, or *percentiles*; in a list of 100 entries the median will be the 50th percentile.

More frequently, four divisions, or *quartiles*, are used. The upper quartile marks the value above which a quarter of the entries fall, and the lower quartile that below which a quarter fall. The difference between the values of the upper and lower quartiles is called the *inter-quartile* range, and half the entries fall within it. Half the inter-quartile range is called the *quartile deviation*.

The mean centre of a population distribution over a surface

If a population (for example, houses, telephone kiosks or homes of civil servants) is distributed over an area such as a town, it may be useful to find the centre of this distribution. If the population is evenly distributed, this will be the geometrical centre of the area they occupy. (If the area were cut out of cardboard and balanced, first along one axis and then another, on the edge of a ruler, this centre would be where the two lines of balance cut.) If the population is not evenly distributed, we need to move away from that centre to allow for the fact that there are more individuals in one part than the other.

To do this we must first divide the area (*see figure* 9) so that the various densities are contained in sub-regions; normally we shall have to use the sub-regions employed for collecting the statistics (for census figures this will probably be wards). On this we superimpose an orthogonal (right-angled) grid. We then assume an even distribution in any individual sub-region, mark the geographical centre of each, and express it in co-ordinates of x and y. Each set of co-ordinates is now weighted by multiplying it by the total population within the sub-area. All the weighted x figures are then added together, as are all the weighted y figures. Each sum is then divided by the total population for the whole area to give the co-ordinates for the centre.

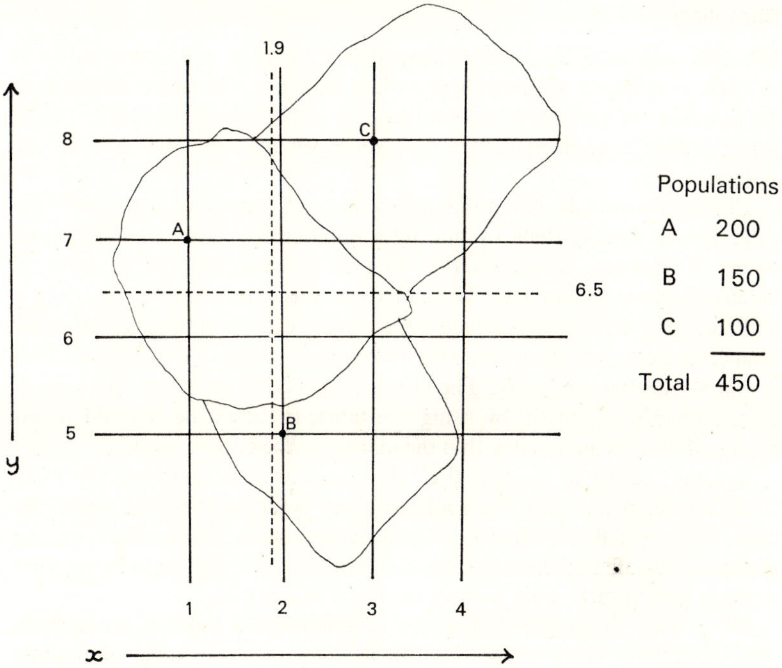

Figure 9

	Weighted x's
A	$1 \times 200 = 200$
B	$2 \times 150 = 300$
C	$3 \times 100 = 300$
	Total 800

	Weighted y's
A	$7 \times 200 = 1\,400$
B	$5 \times 150 = 750$
C	$8 \times 100 = 800$
	Total 2 950

$$\text{Average } x = \frac{800}{450} = 1.9 \text{ approx.} \qquad \text{Average } y = \frac{2\,950}{450} = 6.5 \text{ approx.}$$

Co-ordinates of mean centre 019065

Sampling

We may not have the time or man-power to make a detailed study of the whole town, or we may have to use statistics which are incomplete. In this case we may resort to sampling. A great deal of statistical theory and practice is concerned with this; here we may mention one or two points.

Firstly, we must be able to identify our areas, points, or lines, numerically. This is usually done by putting a numbered grid over the map and using co-ordinates to refer either to grid intersections (points) or grid squares (areas, or patches). We can then select our samples by using a table of random numbers which ensures that every number has an equal chance of being chosen so that the selection is completely unbiased. This is *simple random sampling*. The outline is probably irregular. If a square at the margin is chosen, by using the table, it should be rejected if less than half of it is contained within the margin of the outline.

We may know or suspect that the things we are counting are more likely to be in one area than another, and we may therefore want this area to have a better chance of being represented. In this case we can divide the whole region into suitable sub-areas and apply random numbers to each area in turn. This is *stratified random sampling*.

If we want to sample from a list, or along a line, we may select every *n*th thing (say, every tenth house in a street), using a table of random numbers for selecting our start. This is *systematic sampling*.

How many individuals do we need in our sample? This depends on the size of the universe (the total number of things from which the sample is drawn), the variation inside the universe, the degree of precision required (the tolerance), and the sampling method used. There is therefore no simple answer and resort must be had to a textbook on statistics. It is interesting to note that as the size of the universe increases, the sample size need not increase greatly and therefore the percentage to be sampled drops. On the other hand, in local study the universe is often too small for small samples to be reliable indicators of the nature of the whole.

Matrices

A matrix shows the relationship between two sets of things by entering information in columns and rows. A simple example is a distance chart. We put a number of towns along the top and the same towns, in the same order, down the side; we then enter in the appropriate spaces the distances between each pair of towns. This matrix is symmetrical because the distance *A-B* is the same as the distance *B-A* (unless there is some factor, such as a one-way system, which affects distance in accordance with direction).

Figure 10
An information matrix

	Town Hall	Hospital	Secondary School	Cinema	Post Office	Railway Station
A	1	1	1	1	1	1
B	0	0	1	1	1	1
C	0	0	0	1	1	0

A matrix can also store information about the relationship between things and places. We may have places down one side, identifying rows, and we may have things (for example, a list of functions) along the top, identifying columns. We can then enter along a row the number of each function the place has, or we may simply enter '0' if it has not got it and '1' if it has. A matrix is useful as a store of information but it can also be manipulated (there is a whole mathematics of matrices).

Gravity models

In analysing the geography of a function such as marketing it is necessary to know the area over which this function operates, that is, its sphere of influence. This is a statistic basic to Central Place theory (*see pp. 126–9*). For example, if there is a shop or a hospital or a school, we need to know how far people will come in order to make use of it. This can be discovered empirically by observing what happens in an actual case, but such observations are difficult to make accurately and they have no general application. Is there a general law about spheres of influence which we can apply in all situations?

The answer is that there is no one law which will exactly fit every case, but that there are some which are shown to work fairly well in a large number of situations. The simplest of these is Reilley's 'Law of Retail Gravitation'. This assumes that the attraction between two marketing centres acts in the same way as the gravitational force between two masses. Gravity acts, according to Newton's law, with an effect which is directly proportional to the masses of the two bodies and inversely proportional to the square of the distance between them. If we substitute population for mass we can get a figure for retail attraction by multiplying the two populations together and dividing by the square of the distance.

Given populations P_i and P_j separated by distance d_{ij}, the formula is

$$M_{ij} \text{ (= retail attraction)} = \frac{P_i \, P_j}{(d_{ij})^2}$$

It can be shown that if this is true then we can define the 'break point' between the two centres, the dividing line between those who shop in one centre and those who shop in another. If k is the break point in the following diagram

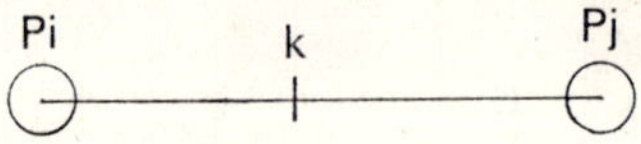

the distance of k from centre j is given by the formula

$$d_{jk} = \frac{d_{ij}}{1 + \sqrt{\frac{P_i}{P}}}$$

where:

d_{jk} = distance of breakpoint (k) from place j
d_{ij} = distance between places i and j
P_i = population of i
P_j = population of j

There is no reason why retail attraction should follow the law of gravity and we may get a better fit to the actual circumstances if we alter our parameters and definitions. For example, cubing may make a better approximation to reality than squaring, as it increases the influence of distance. Also, it is unlikely that figures for total population will give the best result; we may need to re-state population in terms of those actually engaged in marketing. In local study it would be useful to try out Reilley's 'Law' in its crude form, see how far it fitted the observed facts, and attempt various modifications to the formula to see if they make a better approximation.

Communication networks

There are a variety of ways in which networks may be quantified. The simplest is probably to measure the total length of road. This is not very useful, but if we measure the total lengths of different kinds of road, or measure the total lengths in different regions of the town, we have something more meaningful which can be used for comparison. Length in itself, however, is not very significant. It becomes more useful when combined with something else as a ratio—for example,

(*a*) With area to give density—a density map may be made.
(*b*) With traffic to give degree of use.
(*c*) With cost and income to give profitability.
(*d*) With feeder points (e.g. bus stops) to give accessibility.
(*e*) With numbers of inter-connections to give connectivity.

Connectivity can best be approached by expressing a communications system in terms of *nodes*, or *vertices*, joined by *arcs*, or *edges* (but it is possible to have a node with no connections). The connectivity of the system can be measured by the Beta (ß) index which is obtained by dividing the number of edges by the number of nodes. With a given number of nodes the index rises with the number of edges, that is, as connectivity increases.

Another index is the cyclomatic number, *mu* (μ), which is the number of arcs less the number of nodes plus the number of separate systems (*sub-graphs*). The more complex the network, the higher the cyclomatic number.

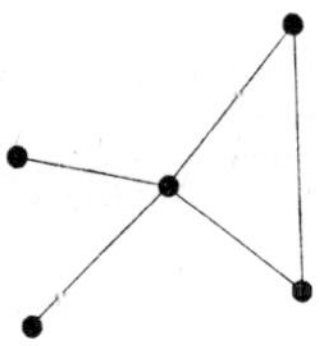

5 nodes ß = 1

5 edges μ = 1

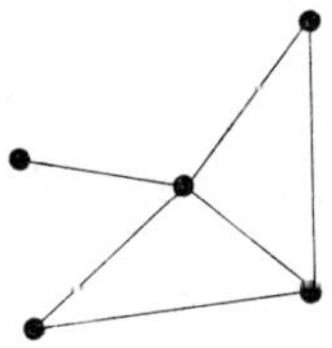

5 nodes ß = 1·2

6 edges μ - 2

An arc also defines two *regions*, one on either side of it. It often helps to clarify a communications system if we re-draw it in terms of nodes, arcs, and regions, adapting distance and direction to make the map more immediately understandable. A well-known example of such a *topological transformation* is the map of the London Underground.

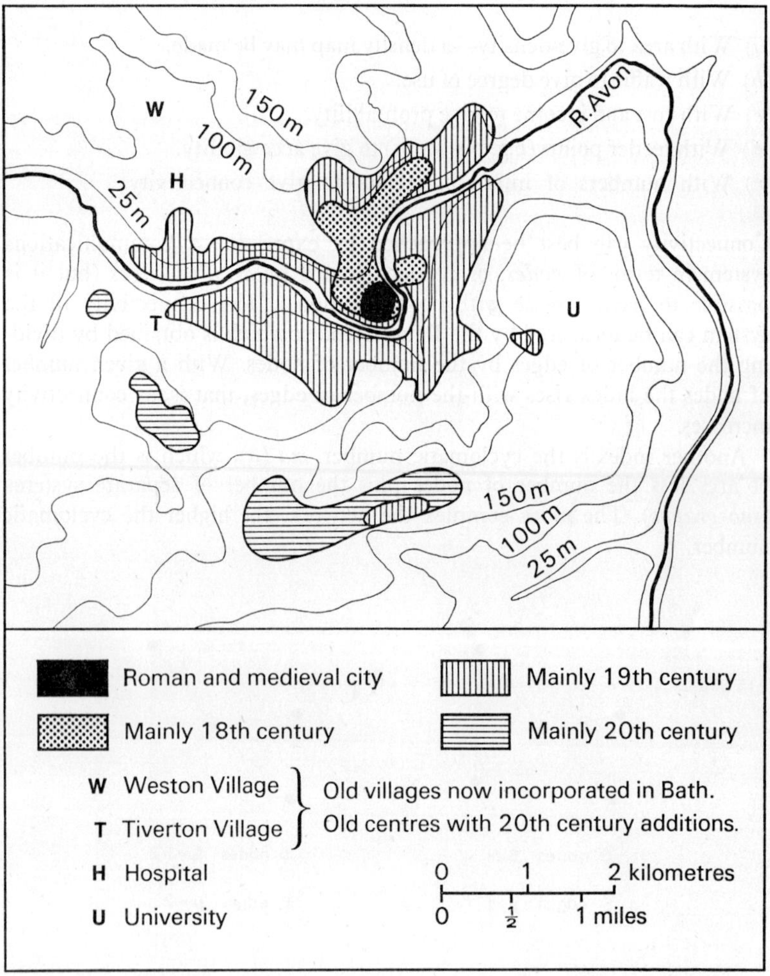

Figure 11 Bath: relationship of growth to relief

6. The geographic base

Relief

Start by studying a relief map. The best is probably the 1 : 25 000 as it has the smallest contour interval and is not too unwieldy in scale. For a very large area a 1 : 63 360 (or 1 : 50 000) map may have to be used, and for a small area it may be possible to copy the contours from the 1 : 25 000 onto the 1 : 2 500 map, using spot heights as a guide. It is often difficult to distinguish contours in the built-up areas and a magnifying glass will help.

Draw a contour map of your town with only the outline of the built-up area and one or two reference points such as outstanding buildings (see figure 11). Take this map to a good vantage point, which may have to be on a building, and, with field glasses if necessary, relate the map to what you see. Study the ground and map for any significant effects the relief may have had on the layout of the town—this may become more evident as further work progresses and you may have to modify your first ideas. Look for any pattern of physical regions, paying particular attention to those physical features which appear to relate to types of building development and communication patterns.

Strengthen contours that mark important breaks in slope, for example those which outline the rim of a plateau-top, the edge of a flood-plain, or the boundaries of a shelf of land. Choose significant lines along which to draw cross-sections (*see figure 12*). It may be helpful to construct a relief model* to which details of the town may be added later. Visit any areas which seem to need further investigation or explanation. Illustrate relief with sketches and photographs.

Even a 5m (or 25ft) contour interval will not reveal small changes in slope which may be of great local importance. These can be recorded by visiting areas and making a street map with arrows having different numbers of barbs according to whether you consider the slope to be flat, slightly sloping, steep, or very steep. If these arrows are drawn to point downhill, patterns of valleys may appear which are not evident from the map but which are important locally with regard to, say, the alignment of streets. The arrows will also show breaks in slope.

If you want to measure the slopes more accurately you can use a level and staff, which would be an expensive and quite lengthy business, as well

* See Haddon, J., *Local Geography*, George Philip, 1964, pp. 75–78.

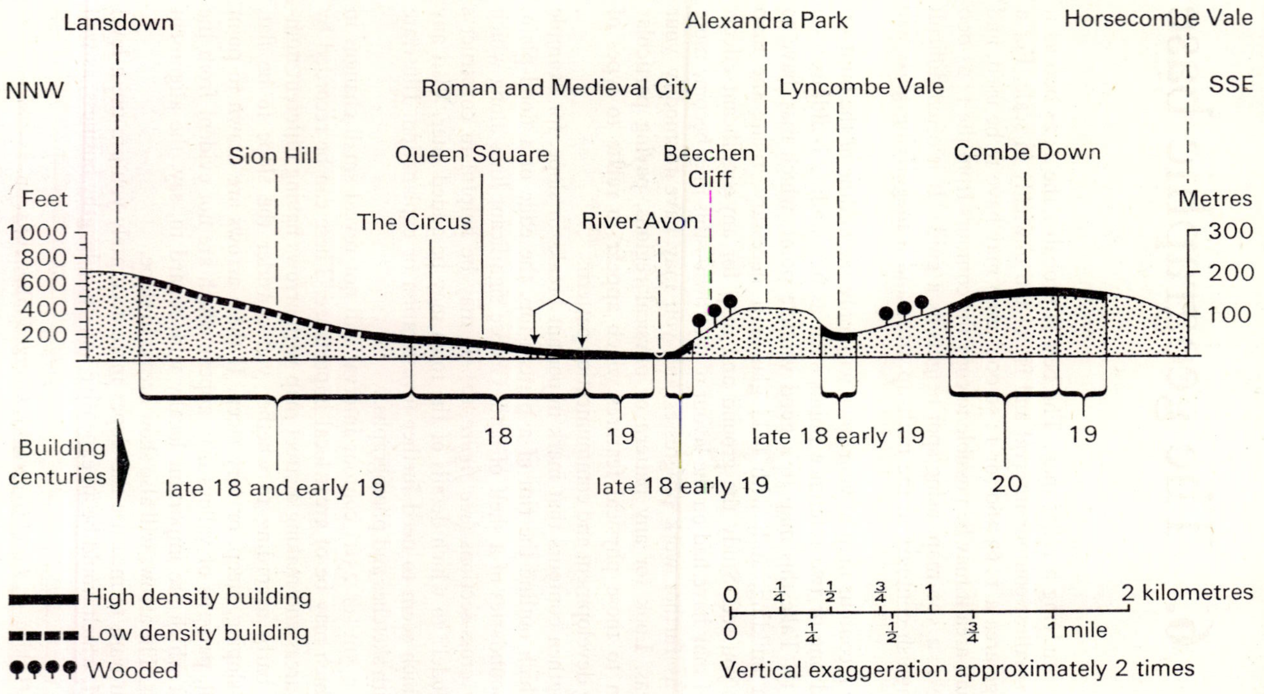

Figure 12 Cross-section of Bath

as unpopular with pedestrians, traffic, and policemen. Alternatively you could use a simple clinometer (*see Appendix 4*).

If you measure shape accurately, you may be interested in the following classification used by the West Midland Group on Post-war Reconstruction:

1 : 7.5 Steeply sloping, unsuitable for development
1 : 7.5 to 1 : 10 Moderate slopes, development undesirable
Less than 1 : 10 Suitable for development

Aspect

An important factor of relief is the direction in which a slope faces—its aspect. A north-facing aspect in the British Isles gets less sun than a south-facing one, and this may affect the orientation of streets and of factory buildings. Aspect is also important in relation to prevailing winds, although it should be noted that streets have a funnelling effect which can cause marked local changes in wind direction. Incidentally, it is useful to carry a compass, not only for observing orientation effects but for simple reference in note-taking to distinguish one side of a street from the other. In using a compass in towns, remember that there is usually a good deal of iron about, including buried pipes, which may affect the compass reading.

Reaction to relief

A straight *description* of relief is inadequate. A town is a man-made thing and relief gains its significance from the way it has affected the human activity of town-building. Unfortunately there is no simple correlation between relief and building for there are many ways in which a physical feature can be treated. Man may react to a steep slope by avoiding it. On the other hand he may build along a contour, or directly up the slope; he may dig into the hillside to make a level platform, or he may get the same result by constructing artificial levels on arches, he may make the back of the house a different height from the front. In some cases, moved by fashion or pride or whim, he may build in a manner totally unsuited to the terrain.

Man's ability to deal with the problems posed by relief will depend to some extent on the state of building technology at the time. Low-lying places may be built up, valleys filled in, rough places made smooth, hillsides terraced. On the other hand, changes in building style may alter requirements—sites suitable for two-storey terraces may be unsuitable for multi-storey blocks.

Whatever the circumstances, the physical nature of the area will have *some* effect and this must be carefully noted, always bearing in mind changing needs, changing methods, changing fashions, and the ingenuity and frequent illogicality of man's activities. Let us study the facts and not be led away by over-simplified generalisation. And let us remember that we shall need to use words. A map or model will show relief, a map or model will show the effects of relief, but only words can *explain* the variety of response.

Generalisations are useful but they must not be made at the expense of ignoring the awkward facts that spoil the tidy pattern. You will probably find that one physical region has been used in more than one way and you may be able to show this by sub-dividing the region, but a more difficult problem arises when a type of development or street-pattern which started in one region has spread to another where it may not be very appropriate. This can be shown by drawing the street land use, or building pattern, on a transparent overlay superimposed on a relief map. This is a useful technique and a series of such overlays, preferably drawn in contrasting colours, can teach us a great deal about the way in which certain features correspond with each other. We must, however, be careful not to assume that because two things occur together, one has necessarily caused the other.

Geology

This is important because:

(*a*) it may relate to the economic activity of the town (presence of coal, salt, iron, fertile farmland etc.).

(*b*) it determines what local building materials are available.

(*c*) it controls the local water supply.

(*d*) it affects the nature of building sites and the type of foundations needed.

(*e*) it helps to explain the relief of the area.

We can either note the effects of geological influence and then work back to the local geology, or we can start with the latter, treating it generally and then concentrating on those aspects which are relevant to the particular town study. The former method tends to lead to 'spotty', disorganised presentation, and the latter, although it may produce some irrelevant matter, is, if handled properly, more satisfactory. Whichever you use, you will need to find out about the rocks of the area. The Geological Survey have done a lot of the work for you, but unfortunately they are unlikely to give you the detail you require for some purposes.

The best way to start, once you have a general idea of the relief and layout of your town, is to study the geological map, published by the Ordnance Survey. The 1 : 10 000 maps may not have been published for your area, as they have been for Inner London, but they may be available for consultation at your local library or at the library of the Geological Museum, Exhibition Road, London S.W. 7. The best map you are likely to have available is the 1:63 360 (the 1:250 000 is useful for general purposes only). If you are in an area with glacial deposits you will need the 'Drift' as well as the 'Solid' edition, but in any case you will need to supplement the map by as much personal observation as possible.

Holes are always being dug in towns and these can provide useful information. Unfortunately such holes often penetrate no further than the 'made' ground and do not disclose the base rock, but even if they do not help you with the solid geology they can assist you in making your own map of man-made deposits. Exploratory bores to check local geology are often made for road-building, water supply, tunnelling, housing, and other purposes. It would be very helpful to talk to the engineers concerned, and the firm might even let you have a list of the sections passed through. Any cuttings and quarries should be studied; drawings and notes should be made of the nature of the rock, the thickness of the strata, and its dip and strike.

For further information, consult the Geological Survey Memoir for your district and any material available in local libraries and museums, including reports of archaeological digs. Newspaper files may give useful information, particularly where new buildings, communications, or water supply are concerned.

Weathering and denudation

An understanding of the way in which the land is moulded by the wearing away of its surface, and by the transport and deposition of eroded material by natural agencies, is necessary if the relief of the area is to be explained. This can be learnt from any standard text on Physical Geography, but there are two points which merit special mention here.

Firstly, erosion, transport, and deposition by human activity may be very important in determining the relief of towns. Large areas of London, for example, have been built on mud dredged out of the Thames; housing estates have been built on rubbish dumps; hillsides have been eaten away by quarries; whole areas have been undermined, sometimes causing subsidence of the surface; transport requirements have resulted in cuttings, tunnels, and embankments. In the historical development of a town, houses have been levelled and new ones built above, so that the present town may lie a metre or more above the original ground. Man may also interfere with natural drainage by embanking rivers, putting streams into pipes, walling slopes, or sealing springs. From personal observation and the study of old maps and newspapers you should be able to draw a useful map of these man-made features, including the made ground referred to above.

Secondly, the surface of a building or a road is as subject to weathering as an outcrop of natural rock, and in the polluted atmosphere of cities it is subject to even stronger chemical attack. The study of weathering in towns is an interesting part of geography which has been rather neglected, and the following notes are therefore included for guidance.

The most commonly affected rock is limestone, and it must be remembered that lime is also a constituent of concrete, cement, mortar, and cast-stone. Limestones are carbonates and they react chemically with rainwater, which is a weak carbonic acid formed by the dissolving of carbon dioxide present in the air. This reaction forms a bi-carbonate which is soluble.

In the polluted air of towns, however, the chief agent is sulphur dioxide which acts on the limestone to form sulphates, whose crystallisation creates strains and causes the rock, or the mortar, to crumble. Dolomite, which is a double carbonate of calcium and magnesium, forms calcium sulphate and magnesium sulphate when in contact with sulphur from the air. Magnesium sulphate (Epsom salts) is easily dissolved, and consequently deep cavities may be formed in the stone.

Evaporation of moisture from porous limestone results in a hard surface deposit, or *scale*, of gypsum (hydrated calcium sulphate). Behind this, conversion of the limestone to calcium sulphate produces a spongy mass which pushes out the surface scale to form blisters.

Damage can also be done by other soluble salts (e.g. salt, or sodium chloride, in sea air) crystallising in the pores of the rock and exerting disruptive pressure. When the product of weathering is soluble or soft the surface of the building will show strong colour contrast between rain-washed and protected areas.

Building stone is also affected by *mechanical weathering*, for example by the sand-blast of on-shore winds and by water freezing in cracks or pores. The latter is particulary noticeable in some stone used for sills and steps. Expansion and contraction with changes in temperature set up strains which may cause cracking, particularly when different materials, with markedly different coefficients of expansion, are closely connected. Similar strains may be set up when materials shrink on drying out.

Damage to brick walls is often caused by sulphate attacks on the lime in the mortar. These sulphates may come from the brick itself and the reaction is rapid when the brick is wet. Not only may the sulphates react with the mortar but they may also crystallise at the surface of the brick itself. On new brick this crystallisation may form as a white deposit, or efflorescence, on the surface. If this is brushed off it will not recur unless water continues to find its way into the brick, in which case continued crystallisation in the surface pores will cause the surface of the brick to deteriorate. Magnesium sulphate is particularly liable to cause this kind of damage.

Mortar is made with slaked lime—that is, quicklime (calcium oxide,

CaO) which has been treated with water to form calcium hydroxal CaC2H). If there are unslaked particles these will react with any moisture which gets into the mortar, expand, and create stresses which may lead to crumbling.

If there is too high a moisture content in the brick, it is, like stone and concrete, liable to shrink when it dries and to cause cracks to form at the joints. Wet brick is also liable to cracking or powdering at the surface when the water in the pores freezes and expands.

Chemical action affects metals, particularly iron which oxidises rapidly to form rust. The downwash of iron oxide may be seen in red streaks on buildings. In some reinforced concrete, rust from the rods embedded in it discolours the surface, while the extra bulk of the oxide may cause the concrete to crack. Similar strains occur in metal-framed windows.

Copper reacts with sulphur dioxide to form copper sulphate, and the resultant green colour is one of the reasons why copper is sometimes used to sheath roofs. Zinc is often used as a protective cover to iron (galvanised iron), because once a surface layer of zinc oxide is formed reaction under it becomes very slow.

The products of decomposition are gradually washed away, but in some cases slow percolation of lime-charged water may lead to crystallisation of calcium carbonate at the surface to form stalactite-like formations. This can sometimes be seen in archways where the water has seeped through limestone or mortar.

A useful reference is *The Weathering of Natural Building Stone*, by R. J. Schaeffer, H.M.S.O., 1931. This is out of print but you may be able to find it in a library. Weathering of brick is dealt with in *Some Common Defects in Brickwork*, National Building Studies Bulletin No. 9, H.M.S.O., 1950, reprinted 1965.

Climate

Climate may affect the function and form of a town. Resorts publish sunshine figures and we are invited to 'bracing Skegness' or 'the Cornish Riviera', and undoubtedly the development of some seaside resorts is linked with the climatic advantage they offer. The damp air of Lancashire had something to do (though far less than is generally believed) with the establishment of the cotton-spinning industry there. Cold, windy regions call for thick walls and narrow streets, and shelter from prevailing winds may help to determine the pattern of residential settlement.

A town, particularly if it is very large, tends to develop climatic characteristics of its own. Covering the land with tarmac and buildings alters the heat balance and the water balance. A town may therefore develop a 'heat island'. Winds will be channelled by streets or slowed down by buildings. Indeed, it is often noticeable how the weather at a given time varies from one part of the town to another.

It will be possible to get some idea of climatic variety inside a town from personal experience, but it is more accurate to obtain instrumental observations, and you may be able to organise these with the help of friends or the co-operation of schools. London has a successful scheme organised by the Department of Geography of University College.

For general information you may be able to find a weather station in your town, possibly run by the Parks Department. It must be emphasised that in a climate as changeable and various as ours, average figures can be very misleading. In any case, for our purposes here, the climate only becomes significant where it is related to the town itself, to its buildings, layout, and activities.

Stream patterns

It is no accident that most of our towns are by streams. They were founded by an invading people who had no maps, and to whom a river valley would be the surest way of penetrating a strange land and which, when they settled, would provide water for their cattle and themselves. Rivers could often transport heavy goods, and led to the surrounding sea. A river crossing was a convenient place to rest and to exchange goods; it acted as a focus of routes and trade, and it could often provide protection for a settlement. Moreover, river plains were often fertile.

There, were, of course, disadvantages. The river might flood, the low lands might be marshy, and they were often heavily wooded. The people who used the valleys needed to know how to overcome these difficulties, and the prehistoric farmers preferred the more open uplands. In general, however, when man had a greater control of his environment he found the river sites attractive, and it is very likely that your town has a river or stream even if it is now of little importance in the life of the place, except perhaps as a sewer. Your town site should be studied carefully in relation to the river, particularly for evidence of firmer and slightly higher ground which would provide protection from flood or firm footing for a bridge; fordability in early times may also have been important in determining the exact position where goods and travellers would cross. If the river is tidal, note should be taken of the tidal limit and the course of the deep-water channel.

Tributary streams will have developed valley patterns which may have been important in focusing routeways or providing sheltered areas for settlement. In the case of ports they may have provided a sheltered haven in early days. Many such streams have been put underground during town development and may only be evident in old maps or in street names.

In studying our streams we should be concerned with the influence they have had in the past on the development of the towns, their present use, and the possible way they may be developed, including any provision for flood-control. Incidentally, the nature of the water itself should not be ignored as it could have an important bearing on industrial processes.

The water-table

Until the late nineteenth century towns derived most of their water supply from local rivers, springs, and wells. To contain water a well must reach below the water-table, the level at which the rock is saturated, and a high water-table may have been an important factor in selecting a settlement site. With more and more water being drawn off, the water-table becomes lowered and many wells run dry. This lowering of the water-table may also have a bad effect on wooden pile foundations, as has recently been found in the case of York Minster. The movement of groundwater may carry pollution into wells, and in the past this has led to ill health in towns. The covering of the ground with impermeable materials, in roads and buildings, may starve the water-table locally, but in times of storm may cause an excessive run-off of surface water which can be dangerous, particularly if the storm drains are inadequate or become blocked.

Where the water-table cuts the surface of the land at the side of a valley, springs may develop and these may have been of importance from quite early times as a source of water supply. Later some of these springs would be used to feed reservoirs from which water would be piped by gravity to the town, mainly to fountains or conduits in the streets. Later again would come the provision of piped water supplies to individual buildings. Until a really efficient pumping system could be developed the supply would be limited by the natural head of water, that is, the height of the reservoir above the delivery points; indeed, tall buildings with modern facilities could not be built until the problems of high-level plumbing had been solved.

With the increased demand for water for both industrial and domestic purposes, towns have had to bring in supplies from some distance away, and the study of the geography of a town would not be complete without some account of its water supply, and the reasons for the siting of reservoirs and the routing of water mains.

Incidentally, bathrooms and water-closets were not common until the end of the nineteenth century. In the older buildings this affects the townscape since these hygienic features were often added as box-like projections to the back.

Information on water supply can be obtained from the Water Boards concerned, the River Authorities, and the Memoirs of the Geological Survey. Local newspapers may have accounts of various new projects.

7. Land utilisation

GENERAL LAND-USE SURVEY

On the geographic base of the town Man has superimposed a pattern of buildings, streets and open spaces. These are the geographical expression of the functions of the town, and by studying them we determine both those functions and also the way in which they have affected the appearance of the place. We are here concerned with ways of collecting this information, but I must once again stress that you should then proceed to judgement. In this case what is to be judged is whether the present arrangements are enabling the town to fulfil its functions in the most efficient way, remembering that one of them is to provide an environment in which it is pleasant to live and work.

The main functions of a town are (*a*) residential, (*b*) commercial, (*c*) industrial, (*d*) administrative, and (*e*) provision of services. The same building may serve for more than one function. For example, a 'parlour' shop is both residential and commercial; a small pottery which sells its wares on the spot is both commercial and industrial; a Town Hall is partly concerned with the adminstration of services. On the whole, however, a rapid survey could be made by travelling through the streets of the town and marking off the five types on a broad general basis, deciding in each case what is the *dominant* land use. There will probably be one area where there is a complicated mixture of shops, offices, and places of entertainment. This is 'downtown', 'Main Street', 'the Centre', or, to adopt a widely used American term, the C.B.D. (Central Business District), and may be classified separately.

This survey will give a general picture of the distribution of functions but will conceal many significant variations within the scheme. If you want more detail, or you are concentrating on a smaller area than the whole town, you will need to make a building-by-building survey, using a more detailed classification. For this there is no universally accepted code. The one I give here was devised by a colleague, Mr. Derek Walkerdene, and myself, and has been found workable and useful as a basis for analysis. It can be modified to suit your particular requirement.

LAND-USE SURVEY CLASSIFICATION AND CODE

Residence

R/T	Houses—terraced
SL	Semi-detached large houses
SS	Semi-detached small houses
DL	Detached large houses
DS	Detached small houses
FH	Flats—high rise
FL	Flats—low rise
HF	Houses converted to flats
B	Bungalows
C	Caravans

Industry
(based on the S.I.C.—Standard Industrial Classification)

I/X	Extractive (mines, quarries, etc.)
T	Textiles
E	Engineering and metal trades
F	Food and drink
D	Dress
C	Chemicals
P	Paper and printing
V	Vehicles
L	Leather
BR	Bricks, pottery, glass, cement, etc.
W	Wood, timber, furniture, etc.
B	Building construction
O	Other (e.g. rubber, plastics)

Commerce

C/SL	Shops—large
SS	Shops—small
D	Department stores, supermarkets
M	Markets
OPu	Offices—public
OPr	Offices—private
B	Banks
W	Warehouses, coal yards, etc.

Other services

S/T	Transport
G	Garages
P	Public buildings, including churches

S	Schools and other educational establishments
U	Public utilities (Gas, Water, etc.)
H	Hotels
I	Inns, cafes, restaurants
R	Recreational and entertainment facilities
O	Other

Open space

O/F	Farmland
M	Market gardens
G	Gardens and allotments
C	Car Parks
R	Recreation grounds and parks
Ce	Cemeteries
W	Water

Unused land

U/W	Waste land
D	Derelict land
R	Land in process of re-development (code for future use can be added)

When making land-use surveys in accordance with the above code, it was found convenient to note features relating to the appearance of the buildings. This could be the subject of a separate survey and is therefore considered in the next chapter. However, since in practice it was found useful to put it on the same recording sheet as land use, details are also given below.

APPEARANCE OF BUILDINGS CLASSIFICATION AND CODE

Age of building

E	Early (could be sub-divided into M = Medieval, T = Tudor)
S	Stuart (to include Jacobean, Carolean and Queen Anne)
G	Georgian
R	Regency
V	Victorian
Ed	Edwardian
I	Inter-war
P	Post-war

Windows

S	Sash
C	Casement

BS Bow, sash
BC Bow, casement
Sl Sliding
F Fixed

Walls

S Stone
B Brick
P Plastered
W Wood
M Metal (e.g. corrugated iron)
C Concrete
O Other

Roofs

Sl Slate
St Stone
T Tile
O Other (e.g. asbestos)

The recording sheet

This enables the use of different storeys to be recorded but does not, of course, cater for very high blocks for which extra information may have to be entered on a separate sheet. Where a tall block has a single use

Street, direction, side.............. Date....................

Recorder.............................. Day............ Time....................

Serial No.	Street No.	Front Garden	Floors								Back Garden	Building				Other Details
			B	G	1	2	3	4	5	6		W'dow	Wall	Roof	Age	

Figure 13

SERIAL NO.	STREET NO.	FRONT G'DEN	STOREYS								BACK G'DEN	BUILDING				OTHER DETAIL
			B	G	1	2	3	4	5	6		Windows	Walls	Roof	Age	
① ↓	CHELSEA ROAD S→N LEFT SIDE															
13		×	×	C/SS	R						✓	S	St	Sl	late 19	Chemist NF/DC
14		×	×								✓					Small
15		×	×								✓					garages
16		×	×	C/SS							✓	Shop	B	T	IW?	Electrical goods H/RR
17		×	×	S/O							✓	Shop	B/faced S	T	"	Launderette S/L
18	outhouses for 19															
19	16	×	?	C/SS	R						✓	Shop/S	St	Sl	late 19	Off-Licence OF/OL
→	PARK ROAD															
20	15	×	?	C/SS	R						✓	Shop/S	St	Sl	1888	Haberdasher C/W
21	14	×	✓	C/SS	R						✓	"	"	T		Grocer G/G
22	13	×	✓	C/SS	R					one	✓	"	"	"		Greengrocer OF/G
23	12	×	✓	C/SS	R					range	✓	"	"	"		Co-op butcher OF/B
24	11	×	✓	C/SS	R						✓	"	"	"		Ironmonger H/I
25	10	×	✓	C/SS	R						✓	"	"	"		Dairy OF/D
→	KENNINGTON ROAD															
27		×	✓	C/SS							✓	Shop	St	Sl	IW?	Fishmonger/Poulterer OF/F

②	CHELSEA ROAD N→S LEFT SIDE															
28		×	×	c/ss							✓	Shop	St	T	late 19	Public House
29	GAP															
30		×	×	c/ss							✓	Shop	St	Flat	IW	Co-op Grocery G/G
31		×	×	c/ss							✓	"	"	"	"	Florist NF/FL
32		×	×	c/ss							✓	"	"	"	"	Ironmonger H/I
33		×	×	c/ss	R						✓	Shop/S	"	"	1965 PW	Grocer G/G
33a		×	×	c/ss	R						✓	"	"	"	"	Watches NF/J
34		×	×	c/ss	R						✓	"	St	SI	late 19	Second-hand furniture H/SH
34a	7a	×	×	c/ss	R						✓	"	"	"	"	Shoe repairs and sales C/BR
35	7	×	×	c/ss	R						✓	"	"	"	"	Greengrocer and fish OF/GF
36	6	×	×	c/ss	R						✓	"	"	"	"	Grocer (empty) G/G
37	5	×	×	c/ss	R						✓	"	"	"	"	Haberdasher C/W
38	4	×	×	c/ss	R						✓	"	"	"	"	Butcher OF/B
39		×	×	c/ss							✓	"	"	T	"	Confectioner OF/C
40	Narrow passage															
41				c/ss							✓	Shop	St	T	late 19	Greengrocer OF/G
42				c/ss	R						✓	Shop/S	St	T	IW?	Sweets and Papers T/N
43				s/o	R						✓	Shop/S	St	T	IW?	Dry cleaners S/L

Figure 14 Land-use recording on a field-sheet: Chelsea Road, Bath
For code, see next section. *Shop/S* — ground-floor large shop windows; other windows sashed.

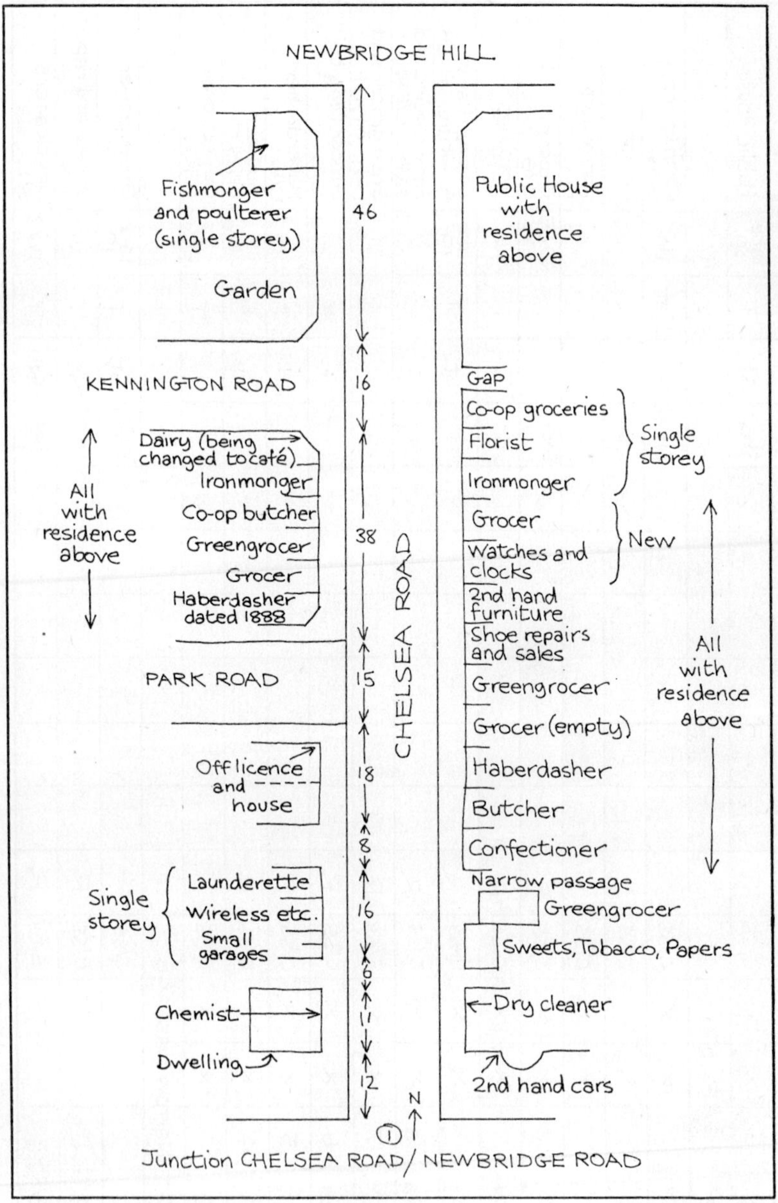

Figure 15 Land-use recording without field-sheet or map: Chelsea Road, Bath
The distances recorded are in paces.

(e.g. flats or offices), it will simply be necessary to put in the use and add a note of the number of storeys.

The form could be extended by the addition of columns for frontage and area; as it was designed to fit lined foolscap sheets these and other refinements were left out.

In recording gardens you need only to put a tick if they exist or a cross if they do not. Where there is an enclosed space which is not a garden (e.g. steps down to a basement), you can put 'A' for 'area'. If it is neither an area nor a garden, but a yard, put 'Y'.

On the form, 'B' is for basement and 'G' for ground floor, to avoid confusion between floors and storeys. In England the second storey is the first floor, whereas in America it is the second floor.

If you have not been able to allocate serial numbers to the buildings it is most important to record the name of the street, the direction you are travelling, and which side of the street you are surveying, e.g. 'Acacia St., S–N, Left'.

Recording with notebook alone

Even without a map or a recording sheet, a useful survey can be made. Draw a line up the centre of the page to represent the street. Write in your starting point at the bottom of the page (e.g. 'South end Cheap St.'). Enter left and right of the line, using the code if possible, the use of each building. The record can be made more map-like by pacing out the frontages on one side of the street and entering the distances at intervals (*see figure 15*). The buildings on the opposite side can be fitted in by referring to the measured ones (e.g. butcher's opposite florist's). For a small stretch of shops you could draw an outline of the façade, number each shop, and write notes about each.

SHOPPING SURVEY

The simplest method would be to take a map into the town and mark on it where every shop was situated, making no distinction between them. There would be some use in this, as the map would show where there were concentrations forming shopping centres, where isolated shops were to be found, and what areas were devoid of shops. Comparison with maps of bus frequencies and housing densities would give some indication of how easy, or difficult, it was for people in different parts of the town to go shopping, and it would show what areas were deficient in shopping facilities. This would, however, give us very limited information, for we would not know what kind of shops we were dealing with.

For a more detailed study we would require a classification of retail establishments, and this is not at all easy to make. There are four main

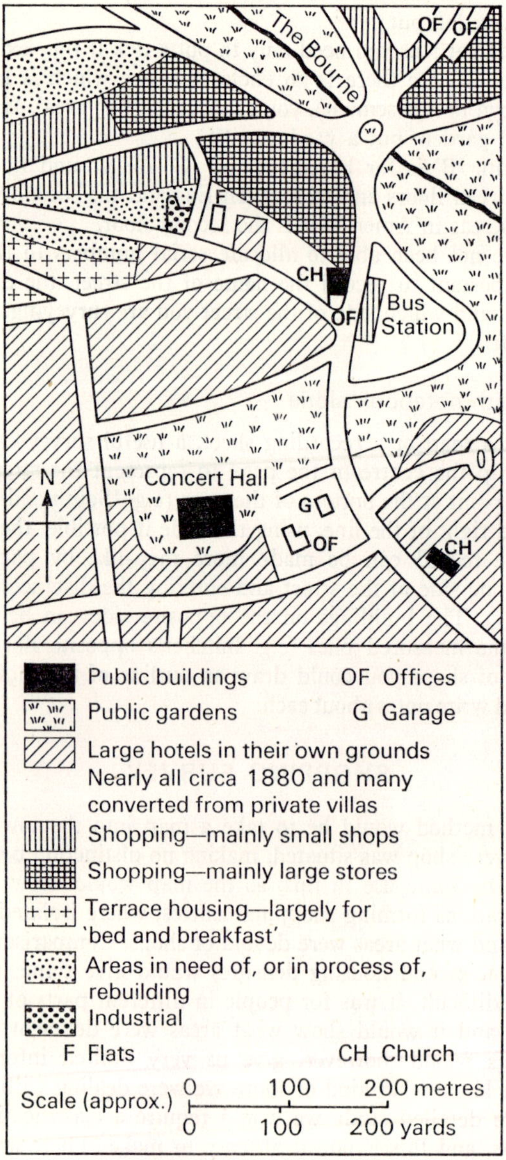
The Bourne
OF
OF
F
CH
OF
Bus Station
Concert Hall
N
G
OF
CH
Public buildings
OF Offices
Public gardens
G Garage
Large hotels in their own grounds Nearly all circa 1880 and many converted from private villas
Shopping—mainly small shops
Shopping—mainly large stores
Terrace housing—largely for 'bed and breakfast'
Areas in need of, or in process of, rebuilding
Industrial
F Flats
CH Church
Scale (approx.)
0 100 200 metres
0 100 200 yards

variables to be considered—what the shop sells, at what price it sells it, what service it offers, and what size the shop is. To this we might add what kind of building it is in.

There are, of course, many shops that sell only one kind of thing. For example there are shops that sell only meat, and we can call them butchers, or only vegetables, and we can call them greengrocers. On the other hand there are shops that sell meat *and* vegetables, not to mention stamps and liquorice all-sorts. There are shops that sell only tobacco, some that sell only sweets, some that sell both, and any of them may, or may not, sell newspapers and/or paperbacks. If we call a shop that sells many things a supermarket, or a multiple store, we still do not know exactly *what* it sells; we would, for example, be bracketing Woolworth's and Marks and Spencer's together. And would we have to classify the village store with Sainsbury's? Obviously the problems of classification are great and it is probably as well to keep to the one worked out for the Census of Distribution. One advantage of doing this is that the Census, which you may be able to consult in your library, gives figures relating to these classes. The figures are given for the whole town but they are useful for finding the relative importance of different types of shops and for comparing them with the figures from other towns. The classification system is as follows, with my own suggestions for code letters.

SHOPPING SURVEY CLASSIFICATION AND CODE
(S.I.C. = Standard Industrial Classification)

Grocers and provision dealers [S.I.C. 820 (1)]

G/G	Grocers
GO	Grocers with off-licences
GB	Grocers with bakery goods

Other food retailers [S.I.C. 820 (2)]

OF/D	Dairymen
B	Butchers
F	Fishmongers, poulterers

Figure 16 (*opposite*) Land-use regions in part of Bournemouth.
Data derived from a one-day survey, August 1967. Note relation of the valley of the Bourne to layout of regions. Historically the first development—late nineteenth century—was of villas on the plateau above. Shopping developed along the streets radiating from the bridging point. Much of the region of large stores was altered or re-built in the nineteenth century. Smaller shops are having difficulty from being in a high-rent area. Behind the main shopping street is an area of decay.

G	Greengrocers, fruiterers
GF	Greengrocers, fruiterers, selling fish
C	Bread and flour confectioners
OL	Off-licences (excluding public houses and shops whose principal sales are of groceries)
O	Other food shops

Confectioners, tobacconists, newsagents [S.I.C. 820 (3)]

T/N	Confectioners, Tobacconists, Newsagents. (Where the sale of newspapers, books and magazines is a major part of the business, the shop is classed as a Stationers.)
C	Confectionery and tobacconists

As I have already mentioned, this is a difficult section. I quote the official note: 'Includes establishments specialising in the sale of confectionery or tobacco or newspapers and periodicals, and those combining the sale of any of these items.' It includes kiosks and railway station stalls.

Clothing and footwear [S.I.C. 820 (4)]

C/B	Boot and shoe shops
BR	Boot and shoe shops which do repairs
MO	Men's outerwear shops
M	Other men's wear shops
WO	Women's outerwear shops
W	Other women's wear, drapers, and general clothing shops

Household goods [S.I.C. 820 (5)]

H/Fu	Domestic furniture
SF	Soft furnishings
FC	Floor coverings
A	Antique dealers
SH	Second-hand dealers
E	Electrical and radio goods
RH	Radio and television hire
RR	Radio and electrical goods shops with repairs
EC	Electrical goods dealer with contracting (Receipts from contracting 20—50% of the total.)
C	Cycles and cycle and motor accessories
CR	Cycle and radio dealers
P	Perambulator shops
I	Ironmongers and hardware shops
Ch	China and glassware
WP	Wallpaper and paint

Other non-food retailers [S.I.C. 820 (6)]

NF/B	Booksellers and stationers
SHB	Second-hand booksellers
Li	Circulating libraries
DC	Dispensing chemists
C	Other retailers of chemist's goods
Ph	Photographic goods
J	Jewellery, watches, and clocks
Le	Leather goods
S	Sports goods
T	Toy shops
F	Fancy goods
Fl	Florists
N	Nurserymen, garden seedsmen
P	Pets and pet food
PB	Pawnbrokers
SH	General second-hand dealers
PO	Sub post-offices with retail sales
O	Other (e.g. retailers of artificial flowers . . . firewood . . . handicraft materials . . . and non-electric sewing machines)

General stores [S.I.C. 820 (7)]

GS/D	Department stores. (Having 25 or more persons engaged in selling, and retailing a wide range of commodities, one of which must be clothing.)
V	Variety stores and bazaars. (Selling a wide range of goods usually displayed in trays or on racks.)
O	Other general stores. (Selling too wide a range of goods to be classed as specialist stores but usually not large enough to be department or variety stores.)

Electricity and gas showrooms

E	Electricity
G	Gas

Service trades [S.I.C. 888-889]

SH/M	Hairdressers and manicurists, including hairdressers/tobacconists
BR	Boot and shoes repairs (not sales)
L	Laundries, launderettes, and dry cleaners

Other classifications

You may find it convenient to alter the above classification by putting together various classes under one heading, by sub-dividing some, or by adding others. For example, all the grocers could be lumped together, all the clothing shops, all types of electrical goods. You might want to distinguish between men's and women's hairdressers. You might want to add children's clothing shops, do-it-yourself shops, and office-equipment shops. You might find it useful to make a separate mention of supermarkets, instead of including them under department stores.

The number of different classes you need to use will also depend on the object of your research. If you want to make a broad study of a large area and present it on small-scale maps, there is no point in collecting more information than you need. A large-scale map of a single shopping street could, by the use of shading or colour for the main headings, and letters for the sub-headings, show the complete classification. A small-scale map of all the shops of a town could only distinguish between about four classes—perhaps Food, Clothing, Household Goods, and Others.

On the other hand, such a general map could be supplemented by large-scale maps of the main shopping centres.

Shops can also be classified according to the prices they charge. Exactly the same branded goods, especially foodstuffs, will be cheaper in some shops than others without there being any difference in the quality of the goods offered. Such small differences are very important to the housewife but would be extraordinarily difficult to record, especially as '3p off X' one week may change to '2p off Y' the next. Differences in prices which reflect the quality of the goods for sale are easier to record, as on the whole a shop tends to be high- or low-priced, rather than offering a very wide range. It is usual to find expensive shops grouped together in one quarter and cheaper shops in another. This price classification is seen in particular with clothing and furniture. By comparing prices a rough classification into E (Expensive), M (Moderate) and C (Cheap) can be made, and a map of the distribution compiled.

The size of the shops depends on their frontage, their ground area, and the number of storeys occupied. The simplest method is to measure the frontages, in metres or feet, on a large-scale map, and to count the number of storeys. With more difficulty the ground area can be measured, or approximated, from the map. Very expensive shops, such as high-class jewellers, tend to be small, as they usually occupy high-cost prestige sites in city centres and do not sell goods in large quantities. On the other hand, the tendency to group different goods under one roof in department stores and supermarkets has led to a great increase in the size of many shops and, in some cases, a consequent move away from the high land values of the middle of large towns.

Classification by goods offered, prices charged, and size of shop can be included on one sheet, as follows:

Street........................ Direction....................

Recorder...................... Date.........................

Ref. No.	Street No.	Distribution Class	Prices	Frontage	Storeys	Name of Shop	Other Details

Figure 17

INDUSTRIAL SURVEY

We have noted a broad classification of types of industry. This is based on the Standard Industrial Classification (S.I.C.) used in the Census of Production which breaks down into a host of sub-divisions. These sub-divisions are published in *Standard Industrial Classification*, H.M.S.O., 1958 (this varies from the 1951 S.I.C.), which you could use for a more detailed survey.

Another very broad division you might use would be between light and heavy industry. Light industry in general has small factories, a small labour force (often largely female), and uses small quantities of raw materials—the radio industry is an example. Light industry is usually less noxious than heavy industry—such as steel making—which tends to need more plant, have a large labour force, predominantly male, use heavy and/or bulky raw materials, require considerable power resources, and produce large, heavy objects. A consideration of the siting of light and heavy industries, their effect on the surroundings, and the suitability of their location would be a useful geographical exercise.

The study of location is basic to geography. A separate map of the distribution of each type of industry should be made, and it may also be useful to map industries that form inter-related groups—small firms, for example, supplying specialist goods to large concerns. It will be helpful to know the date of foundation of each firm and this will enable us to locate areas of new and old industries. Past location may be found from old maps and directories.

Location factors

Requirements of labour, raw materials, power, and suitable building land help to determine where an industry will develop, but there are other factors which merit consideration.

(*a*) *Market orientation*

A town is itself a market for some of its own industries, particularly for household goods, food, and clothing, and this may attract firms into the area. An industry which supplies mainly the town market is said to be 'non-basic', while one which sells mainly outside is 'basic'.

Established industries also tend to attract others which supply them; for example a textile industry will tend to encourage engineering firms, which supply special machinery, and chemical firms, making dyes and bleaches, to move into the area. One of the reasons for the Vauxhall plant moving to Luton was the presence there of the West Hydraulic Engineering Company, with which it later amalgamated.

(*b*) *Financial inducements*

Local and national governments can influence the location of industry by offering financial inducements, such as low-interest loans and special economies in rent and rates. Trading estates may be set up and factory buildings offered on attractive terms. An interesting example was the attraction of foreign industrialists to the 'free port' area within the perimeter of Shannon airport.

(*c*) *Planning policy*

The need to obtain planning permission for the establishment or extension of factories, of the siting of new ones, means that planning authorities can influence the location of industry in the area. This can be seen in the 'zoning' shown on the Town Map. Location of industry is also affected by its need to obtain an I.D.C. (Industrial Development Certificate) from the Department of Trade and Industry.

(*d*) *Strategic considerations*

These may result in an isolated position for some factories, and caused a certain amount of migration of industry during the Second World War, for example to small towns in the West of England.

(*e*) *Decline of an industry*

This releases a labour force and possibly sites and buildings for new concerns.

(*f*) *Accidental factors*

The birthplace of a man of genius, such as Lord Nuffield, may determine the place of origin of an industry. A holiday connection may lead to the idea of an industrial development—light industry at Weston-super-Mare is in part due to the availability of cheap, flat land, but also to the familiarity of Midland workers with the town as a holiday resort. When a firm moves to a new site, or establishes a branch factory, a certain proportion of skilled operatives and management will probably have to move as well, and the move is more likely to be successful if the new area is already known, or is not too far from the original home.

Location and site

In analysing the geography of an industry, we must consider general factors which cause the industry to be *located* in the area, and particular factors which determine exactly where in that area it is *sited*. Thus the presence of local salt supplies may have been a major factor in the location of a chemical industry, but the position of cheaper land and accessibility to routeways may have determined its siting.

We must also remember that the *original* causes may no longer operate; indeed, advantages may become hindrances, as when a central position prevents further expansion, or where a good location for the use of a railway may be a bad one for road transport. There is however a strong tendency (industrial inertia) for an industry to continue where it started, even on the same site, in spite of growing inconvenience. There will be capital, possibly a great deal, tied up in the buildings and plant; there will be a local labour force; there may be special local educational facilities; there are probably ancillary services; and the name of the place may have a marketing value. This means that the present site may only be explicable in historical terms and that we shall have to turn to historical sources such as local histories, old maps, newspapers and directories, and old records of the firm.

Changes in site

If an industry moves within a town, or if—more usually—new industry comes in, a variety of factors may affect the decision. Amongst these are changes in local initiative; changes in local attitude; new sources of raw materials; alterations in transport needs (e.g. from railway to road) and in transport pattern (e.g. the building of a by-pass); engulfment of industrial sites by residential development; changes in technique of production; and development of new industries needing new and different facilities.

Density of industry

This can be shown by superimposing a grid over the location map and calculating, either the proportion of land in each square given over to industry, or the number of industrial workers employed there. The map could then be shaded or coloured to a scale suitable to the range of densities. A fairly good impression might be given by a simple dot map, with a dot for each establishment, although it would be better to grade the dots according to the size of the works represented.

Relative importance of different industries

Importance is difficult to define and cannot necessarily be measured by the number of times an industry appears—how many bakeries, for instance, equal one steelworks? Usually assessment is based on three things:

(*a*) the physical size of the enterprise
(*b*) the number of people it employs
(*c*) the amount of profit it makes

There are also the questions of the level of wages in the industry, and the extent to which other industries depend on it (for example, a motor-car works is often a market for a large number of specialist firms).

Probably the most significant feature for the purpose of urban survey is the proportion of the total labour force of the town which it employs. These figures are given in the Census of Production, although not for individual firms. The proportion can be compared with the national proportion. For example, in the 1961 Census the total labour force in the U.K. was given as 23 616 000, of which there were employed in metal manufacturing 346 110 males and 180 990 females, a total of 527 100 or just over 2.2% of the total. In any town with a greater proportion than this, metal manufacturing is more important in terms of employment than it is in the nation as a whole. The national percentage divided by the local percentage gives a figure known as the *location quotient.*

Transport and industry

Another worthwhile study would be of the amount of traffic involved in an industrial undertaking, and this could be done by traffic counts. Such traffic includes not only lorries and vans, but also the cars and feet of the employees; factories are needing more and more car-parking space, and in America, General Motors reckons on a ratio of one car for every 1.2 employees.

Industrial archaeology

You may have in your town industrial buildings, or their remains, which are no longer used for their original purpose. These fossils of a past industrial age, although by their physical presence geographical, are particularly in the field of study of Industrial Archaeology. For methods of study and recording, consult the *Handbook of Industrial Archaeology,* by

Kenneth Hudson, John Baker, 1967, and the regional books in the Industrial Archaeology series published by David and Charles.

Individual factories

So far we have been considering industry in general, but it is also useful to study the individual geographical expressions of industrial activity, the single factories. In such a study we are concerned with the technical processes of production only in so far as they help to explain the geography of the factory—its location and appearance. We can consider a factory as an assembly point for various inputs (raw materials, labour, power, etc.), and a dispersal point for products (which may be finished or part-finished). Between these two functions lies the function of adding value to the inputs by the processes of manufacturing. These processes will determine the size and nature of the buildings, and their layout. The three aspects, input, process, and output will be largely (though not entirely) responsible for the location and siting of the factory.

In studying a factory it is useful to have some sort of ordered questioning and the following is offered as a guide—it will need modification for particular circumstances.

FACTORY QUESTIONNAIRE

Name of recorder and date
Name of firm Head office of firm
Address and map reference of factory
Other factories and establishments owned by firm, if any
Working floor-space (area)
Storage space (area) for inputs
Storage space (area) for outputs
Sketch-map (*separate paper*) of layout of buildings
Flow diagram of materials between and through buildings
Building materials of factory
Age of buildings
Is it pleasant to look at?
Does it give off unpleasant smells, water-borne effluent, smoke, noise?
How far away are these effects noticeable?
Description of site
Is it easy/difficult of access to vehicles?
Has it good/fair/poor parking facilities?
Why was this site chosen?
What are its advantages/disadvantages?
Where is the nearest factory of the same type?

How many floors are there in the factory?
How is the factory lit?
When was the factory founded?
Were the buildings used for anything before?

Inputs

Source of power
Source of water
Power consumption per year
Water consumption per year
Raw materials
Sources of raw materials
Route of raw materials
Method of transport of raw materials
Does the factory buy any ready-made or semi-finished goods to use in its products (e.g. steel plates, car bodies, small motors)?
If so, where do they come from?
Number of employees—male: female: total:
Where do employees live?
How do they get to the factory?
Arrange the following in order of cost in a year: raw materials, power, labour, rent, rates, transport

Output

What does the factory produce?
Where are the products sent?
How are they transported?
Does the factory advertise its goods?
If so, over how wide an area?
Are products sold direct to general public? To wholesalers? To other firms as raw materials? To shops?
Are any products exported?
If so, where to and by what routes?

Miscellaneous

Were there any Government incentives for establishing a factory there?
Did the firm have to obtain an I.D.C. (industrial development certificate)?
Is there a canteen?
Do the workers have to wear special clothing?
Where is this kept?
Has the factory got a training scheme?
What changes, if any, are taking place at the factory (e.g. enlargement, new products, new techniques)?
For how long is the factory working each day?

REFERENCES

Freeman, T. W., *Geography and Planning*, Hutchinson University Library, 1967.

First published in 1958 and slightly revised since, this book has a useful chapter on the problems of industrial location.

Haddon, J., *Local Geography: Geographical survey in rural areas*, George Philip, 1964.

This includes a short questionnaire for use in studying a factory and has a discussion of some of the more usual location factors.

Hall, P. G., *The Industries of London since 1861*, Hutchinson University Library, 1961.

An interesting study of the forces affecting industrial location, and their results.

Martin, J. E., *Greater London: an Industrial Geography*, Bell, 1966.

Well worth studying, not only for the information about London but also for the methods and mapping used, and the information about siting factors for particular industries. It also contains a lucid account by Colin Brown of industry in the New Towns of the London area.

8. Buildings

MATERIALS

The appearance of a town will naturally depend a good deal on the materials used in the buildings. We have only to think of Bath stone, Westmorland slate, Cornish granite and Midland brick, to realise how much the differences in appearance of Bath, Bowness, Bodmin, and Birmingham owe to their different building materials. In some cases the same material is used consistently throughout the town; more frequently it varies and gives a different appearance to different parts of the place. Thus in Bristol the substantial middle-class Victorian suburbs in Pennant sandstone contrast with their meaner working-class contemporaries in red brick. Change, possibly improvement, of appearance with change of material is the subject of the old rhyme about John Nash:

> Augustus of Rome was for building renowned,
> And of marble he left what of brick he had found.
> But is not our Nash, too, a very great master?
> For he found us all brick, and he leaves us all plaster.

The use of plaster, paint, roughcast, pebble-dash and other masking materials must be noted, for it is the outward appearance of the building we are concerned with, and a house of brick and a house of stone can look identical if they are both covered in white-painted stucco.

A geography of the building materials of your town would record their distribution, their use, and their effect on the appearance of the place. It should then go further, deal with the sources of the materials and attempt to account for their use.

Sources of materials

Until the coming of the railways in the mid-nineteenth century, most building materials, being heavy and bulky, were from the immediate locality. Where water transport was available, or where some particularly important building project was in hand, materials might be brought in from outside, but this was not usually the case. The use of these older materials can therefore be related to the local geology and, if the material is still being used, it may be helpful to consult local quarrymen and builders.

With improved transport, other materials, especially brick, could be brought in relatively cheaply, and you may find a change in material coinciding with transport improvements. Other changes have come with the development of new building techniques. Steel-framed buildings (the first major one in Britain was the Ritz hotel in 1904) carry the weight of the floors and roof on their skeletons and do not need load-bearing walls. It is therefore possible to use panels of light material, or glass, as 'cladding'. Improvements in concrete at the end of the nineteenth century, especially its strengthening with steel rods to form reinforced concrete, led to its more widespread use. The invention of the breeze block, a pre-cast, hollow building brick of coke, clinker, or other waste material, made it the normal walling for small houses after the Second World War, although it does not affect the appearance because it has to be faced with some other material. Artificial stone was invented in the 1770's (Coade stone), and various plasters, notably stucco, were developed to cover walls in the nineteenth century, but there has been a great increase in the use of artificial stone as a facing to ordinary houses since the war. Another change, which tends to make for uniformity, is the increasing amount of pre-fabrication, where large units are factory-assembled and transported to the building site.

Roofing materials are mainly slates, lead, or tiles of stone, clay, or concrete, although modern flat-topped buildings usually have a bituminous cover. All these are heavy, and in the past stone tiles were used in the limestone areas, slates in the regions of metamorphic rocks, and tiles in clay country. Thatch, of reed or straw, which was common in towns in medieval times, had always been a great fire-risk. In 1212, for instance, King John ordered all thatched houses in London to be plastered, and all roofs in future to be of tiles, shingles (wooden tiles), boards, or lead. This order, like many others up to the Great Fire of 1666, was not effective, but by the eighteenth century thatch had become uncommon in towns. The effect of the railways was to make the use of slate and a greater variety of tile much more widespread, and it led to much more variety of roof colour in any one town. Since the 1930's concrete tiles have become increasingly used.

Laws against certain types of construction, such as timber framing, have had some effect. For example, in 1784 George III put a tax on bricks. The result was that many builders faced walls with 'geometrical' tiles, hung to imitate brickwork. The practice went out of fashion with the repeal of the tax in 1850. Another well-known example was the Window Tax, first put on in 1695 and not repealed until 1851. This certainly caused a certain amount of blocking up of old windows and omitting of new ones, but in many cases blocked windows were never intended to have glass but were put in for the sake of symmetry. Glass is, of course, an important building material, but until the nineteenth century it was expensive and could only be produced in small pieces. Then in the 1830's new inventions made glass available more cheaply, in larger quantities, and in big sheets—in time for the Crystal Palace, the great railway stations, and innumerable Victorian conservatories.

Building, especially of the traditional sort, calls for a great deal of wood. In medieval times the timber-framed houses would usually be constructed of local hardwoods, mainly oak and elm, but by the eighteenth century the most widely used wood was, as it is now, the softwood pine or fir, commonly called 'deal', imported then from the Baltic countries and now from the Baltic and Canada. This requires good transport from a port, and it is not surprising that it was a timber merchant who, at the time of Bath's great building expansion in the eighteenth century, was responsible for making the Avon navigable from the port of Bristol. Wood is also used as facing material. The old weatherboard, or clapboard, walls of horizontal overlapping boards was usually of cleft oak but are now more usually of sawn deal.

Although some wrought-iron work may have been produced by local smiths, most of the iron and steel in buildings, including cast iron used for drainpipes, will have come from factories well placed for obtaining coal and ore. Structurally, cast and wrought iron were important during the nineteenth century but towards the end of that period began to be superseded by steel, the production of which was even more narrowly localised.

Finally, it should be remembered that any complete study should include the materials used for roads and pavements. Although the majority of roads are now of tarmac and paving stones of concrete, there are many examples still of cobbles, granite setts, wooden blocks and natural stone paving.

REFERENCES

Bowley, M., *Innovations in Building Materials,* Duckworth, 1960.

Deals with nineteenth- as well as twentieth-century inventions and developments.

Clifton-Taylor, A., *The Pattern of English Building,* Batsford, 1962.

This is particularly useful on materials and their location.

Davey, N., *Building in Britain,* Evans, 1964.

A very interesting study of British architecture from the point of view of building methods and materials.

O'Neill, H., *Stone for Building,* Heinemann, 1965.

Mainly concerned with use and presentation, but has useful descriptive sections.

ARCHITECTURAL STYLE

A map of building materials, with a description of the different types, will tell us a good deal about the appearance of a town, but the description would be incomplete without some indication of the architecture of the buildings themselves. The style of building depends upon the materials available, the state of building technology, the function of the building, and the prevailing fashion in architecture. In any age influences produce standard forms which, in spite of differences in detail, can be recognised over whole areas of the town, and can be usefully mapped and described by using type-labels. Such labels are related to historical periods (e.g. Georgian), to influential architects (e.g. Wren), or to characteristics of the style itself (e.g. Baroque).

As we shall see, type-labels will serve us well until the Victorian and present ages, when the major part of the reconstruction and expansion of our towns took place. In this we are faced with four problems. Firstly, there was no one dominant style; secondly, there was a strong tendency to mix styles; thirdly, there was a tremendous increase in small-house building; and fourthly, no definitive classification has been evolved. We will consider this further in the appropriate sections below, where we outline a brief chronology of styles.

It is not possible here to give more than a skeleton outline, and it is important that you take some trouble to read more about architecture. An important part of Geography is description, and it is remarkable, when so much of the human environment is made up of buildings, that so few geographers have any training in the history of architecture.

There is still much work to be done in this field. In the past, the architectural historian has tended to concentrate on individual, large, 'important' buildings, and you will find therefore that many books have little to say about the majority of buildings in your town. The attitude is changing, but even such a recent book as the Penguin *History of English Architecture* devotes nearly half its photographs to churches, and out of a hundred and seventy-nine illustrations has a mere half-dozen which can be related to the ordinary urban environment. You can do real pioneer work in studying and classifying the building styles of your town.

The brief chronological account that follows, which is based on the list on page 50, is an introduction to the main building styles. It should be supplemented by reference to books on architecture such as those mentioned on pages 80-81. The technical terms used can be found in the next section ('Architectural Vocabulary') of this chapter or in any dictionary of architecture.

Early 1000–1500

This very long period has been treated as one section because very few buildings have survived from it in towns, and it does not form any large part of today's towns. Where it has survived it will probably be in the form of a church, an old town hall, the remains of a castle, or of a town wall and/or gatehouse. Such relics, because of their antiquarian and tourist interest, are usually dealt with in guides and these should be consulted. When a building has lasted for a long time it has usually been modified several times and no attempt should be made to date it by reference to a single feature.

Tudor 1485–1600

Henry VII, 1485–1509; Henry VIII, 1509–1547; Edward VI, 1547–1553; Mary, 1553–1558; Elizabeth I, 1558–1603.

A period of expanding trade, this was a time when much town-building took place, of which only a little has survived. Typical of many areas was the timber-framed, gabled house, thatched, and with over-sailing upper storeys. The timbers themselves might be richly carved and the lath-and-plaster, or brick infilling covered with plaster, might itself be decorated. Windows tended to be large, and bay windows and oriels were popular. Stone buildings had stone mullions and transoms to windows, with drip-stone mouldings (labels) above. Arches were broad and flattened, chimneys tall, ornamental, and often twisted. Strapwork and curved gable ends show influence from the Netherlands, as does the very greatly increased use of brick. Renaissance influence, which took a hundred years to reach England, may be shown by Classical ornament in the form of pillars, pilasters, pediments, and parapets (often pierced or balustered).

Jacobean 1600–1620

Latin Jacobus *for James I, 1603–1625.*

Similar in many ways to the preceding style, in this period there was an increased use of Classical features and a strong tendency towards symmetry. Brick continued to be increasingly used; indeed King James, in a proclamation of 1605, required all persons to build '. . . theire front and windows either of brick or stone as well for reasons of decency as by reason that all great and well grown woods are much spent and wasted, so as timber for shipping waxes scarce'. Strap ornament tended to give way to formalised foliage. Pillars were more frequently used. Windows tended to be rather smaller.

This style continued through the reign of Charles I (1625–49), but at the same time a truly Classical style was introduced by Inigo Jones (1573–1652) who was Surveyor of the King's Works from 1615 to the outbreak of the Civil War in 1642. He had visited Italy and there acquired an admiration for the work and writing of Andrea Palladio (1518–1580) whose 'Palladian' style he introduced into England. Although a great figure in architectural history, his influence during his life did not extend widely and had little effect on the mass of building in the country. Over half a century later, however, his works were to have an immense influence on Georgian architecture. Because of his reputation a large number of buildings have been ascribed to him with which he had no connection.

Carolean 1649–1688

Latin Carolus, *for Charles. Covers reigns of Charles II, 1649–1685, and James II, 1685–1688. Sometimes called* Late Stuart.

During the Civil War and Commonwealth there was little in the way of building, but the Restoration, with its more settled times and a King with a lively interest in Science and the Arts, saw a revival. This was the period of the great rebuilding of London after the fire of 1666, and of the genius of Christopher Wren (1632–1723). The Classical style was now definitely the accepted form, though, as far as the bigger buildings were concerned, in a less severe, freer, and more ornamental style than Palladianism would have allowed. It is sometimes called *English Baroque* but has far less flourish, curve, and fancy than Continental examples. The hipped roof became popular, and projecting eaves were often filled in underneath with wooden cornices, perhaps decorated with modillions. A large triangular central pediment was often used, as were pediments, curved or triangular, and often broken, over doors and windows. Cupolas were a favoured feature. Brick continued to be widely used, often with white stone dressings at the edges and around windows. The round-headed window with small leaded panes was typical of the period.

Queen Anne 1689–1714

This is often taken to include not only the reign of Anne, 1702–1714, but also the preceding reigns of William and Mary, 1689–1694, and William III, 1694–1702.

The characteristic Queen Anne house was of a simple Classical type—hipped roof; wooden cornice, usually painted white; dormer windows, often with their own little pediments; a squarish building in brick, with stone quoins, windows with simple pediments or else flat brick arches, and long-and-short brickwork at the side, often slightly raised or in darker brick. A considerable change in appearance was made by the introduction of sash windows in this period, with their small panes and thick wooden glazing bars. Doorways almost always had canopies, supported on brackets, the shell-hood being a favourite form.

This must not be confused with the 'Queen Anne house' popularised by Norman Shaw (1831–1912), which was something of a mixture of styles of Dutch and William-and-Mary origins.

Early Georgian 1714–1760

George I, 1714–1727 and George II, 1727–1760.

This was the great period of the Palladian revival, led by Lord Burlington (1694–1753) and Colen Campbell (died 1729). Design was according to strict rules, particularly with respect to proportion in relation to the use of the Classical Orders. Balance and order, quiet good taste, and the avoidance of excess in ornament, were the rule of the day.

Gables were unfashionable, and everywhere was to be seen the flat, parapeted skyline hiding the low-pitched roofs, often double saddle-backs like an inverted W. A row of houses might have their fronts combined to form a single, palace-like façade, or be simply a repetition of narrow fronts with perhaps nothing more in the way of ornament than a simple pediment to each door, but saved from dullness by the perfect proportion. Usually the houses would have a basement, lit from small 'areas' in front between the house and the built-up road, and possibly crossed by a flight of steps to the front door. The tallest windows, now all sashed, would usually be on the first floor, the important one or *piano nobile*, while the ground floor might be given a more massive appearance by rustication. Over the door might be found a semi-circular fanlight, although this was more common in the later period, and early in the century doors and windows might be surrounded by bolection moulding. Venetian windows were also a popular feature of this period.

Decoration, apart from pediments, some curved in the earlier period but mostly triangular, was mainly by pillars, pilasters, simple horizontal mouldings, and carved cornices below the parapet, which itself might be decorated with stone urns. Frequently giant columns were used, combining two storeys into one.

Late Georgian 1760–1811

George III; sometimes extended to include Regency.

In reaction to the rather heavy regularity of Palladianism, a lighter, more fanciful, more decorative style developed, associated particularly with the Adam brothers, Robert (1728–92) and James (1730–94). Their two other brothers, John and William, worked with them, but little is known of them. The basic pattern was still Classical but tended to be lighter in construction. Decoration in the form of paterae and Vitruvian scrolls, and ornamental urns in round-headed, shallow niches, were common. Round-headed doorways and ground-floor windows were character-

Half-timbered houses. Burford, Oxon. The parapet, original sash windows, and wooden pilasters of the centre house suggest that it is a little later than its neighbour. The shop fronts are modern. Note the differences in the roofing materials.

Three building periods. King Street, Bristol. The little grey range of almshouses date from the Commonwealth. The white building is eighteenth-century, with some alterations to the ground-floor windows, while its neighbour and the two tall buildings are all post-war.

Queen Anne period.
No. 6, King Street, Bristol.
This house of plastered brick was built about 1700. Note the shell hood, fanlight, string courses, quoins, and structure of the roof.

Regency. Brunswick Terrace, Brighton. Note the simplicity and lightness of the design, the use of stucco, the iron balconies, and, at the side, the semi-circular bay. Pillars and pilasters are of the Corinthian order. The topmost attic windows are a new addition and alter the proportions of the building.

istic; glazing bars became very thin, and large fanlights with thin iron tracery were common. Stucco became popular (there was an 'Adam's new invented stucco') and much of the decorative work was in this rather than in stone. Carvings were also made in Coade stone, a terra-cotta manufactured at Lambeth. Wrought-iron balconies became a feature.

During this period there was a revived interest in Gothic forms, but this did not have a wide influence at the time and was mostly confined to 'follies', although here and there we find 'Gothick' features, such as pointed arches to window frames and battlements to parapets.

Regency 1811–1820

The Prince Regent became George IV, 1820–1830, and was succeeded by his brother, William IV, 1830–1837. The term Regency is sometimes used to cover the whole of the period, in the same way as Georgian is often taken to relate to the reigns of all the Georges and of William.

Although still basically Classical, the whole effect departed more and more from the old forms. Stucco became standard treatment for walls; colonades were in favour; wrought- or cast-iron balconies became more and more slender; bay windows, often semi-circular and running the whole height of the wall were popular; bow-windowed shopping streets were designed and arcades introduced. Windows were often set in shallow, round-headed recesses (depressed arches). There was a greater, more informed, interest in Greek architecture as opposed to Roman. Greek Revival houses tended to be rather squat, with low-pitched pediments, often rectangular, and heavy, usually fluted, columns. Perhaps the best-known monumental Greek Revival building is the British Museum (1823–47), designed by Robert Smirke (1780–1867).

Towards the end of the period an 'Italianate' style developed, particularly for suburban villas, distinguished by low-pitched slate roofs, wide eaves, no basement (although there might be cellars), and often an asymmetrical tower. On the other hand, Gothic detail continued to increase, and there was an interest in Eastern patterns, as in the Brighton pavilion (1815) designed by John Nash (1752–1835). Gothic became the standard form for the new churches in the expanding towns which followed the Church Building Act of 1818.

Victorian 1837–1901

This long period is one where the type-label is not helpful, owing to a profusion of styles which were themselves copies, mixtures, and adaptations of previous ones. Thus we have the Gothic Revival with pointed and ogee arches, towers, pinnacles, battlements, crockets, thin pillars, barge-boarded gables, and wild carving—not necessarily, but not infrequently, all together—applied to suburban houses, town terraces, and public buildings alike; we have Greek Revival (less popular after 1850), with massive pillars beneath heavy entablatures and large triangular pediments, their tynpanums filled with sculpture—a favourite for banks and town halls; we have Venetian Gothic, popular after the public had absorbed and misinterpreted Ruskin's *Stones of Venice* (1851), and characterised by its 'streaky bacon' polychromatic style of bands of coloured brick, high-pitched roofs, and pointed window arches, often in pairs, resting on thin pillars with elaborately carved capitals.

Queen Victoria's fondness for Balmoral Castle (built 1850) gave a certain popularity to 'Scottish Baronial' with its conical-roofed round turrets, while her house at Osborne, Isle of Wight, with its tall rectangular towers and spreading eaves, gave an added attraction to the Italianate style. Nor was what has been unkindly called 'Jacobethan' forgotten. Favoured for country houses and town 'semis', its stone-mullioned oriel and bay windows, curved gables, and strapwork are to be found in many areas and for some public buildings, including railway stations.

And so the list could continue—'Loire chateau', 'Roman Triumphal', 'Neo-Baroque'—you name it and the Victorians could build it. Moreover, in the 'mixed' or 'eclectic' style, they would put them together for you in the same building. Although the various styles are most eye-catching in the large buildings, from breweries to banks, they are clearly evident in many a town and suburban house, and not least in the rapidly growing ranks of the new seaside boarding houses.

Towards the end of the century, largely due to the influence of William Morris (1834–96), Norman Shaw (1831–1912) and C. F. A. Voysey (1857–1941), there came a movement to emphasise craftmanship and the use of good, plain, 'honest', and relatively unadorned materials (Voysey had a preference for white rendered walls, but these were kept plain). There was a tendency to white woodwork, brick, a varied window pattern, often including round windows, prominent and often complicated roof patterns, prominent chimney stacks, and a vaguely Jacobean look.

Another later style can also be traced to the work of Morris, although it was mainly a Continental product and started in Belgium. This was *Art Nouveau* which enjoyed a brief popularity from about 1893 to 1905. It was a style of ornament rather than of architecture, and was distinguished by long, drawn-out, thin forms, curved and intertwining. They were often based on vegetable forms, and tulips were particularly popular. These decorations might be incorporated in stained glass, on tiles, in metal strips, or on beaten copper panels.

The romanticism, individualism, and ostentation of the Victorian Age, coupled with reaction against Georgian uniformity, led to a wild diversity of 'neo' styles sitting cheek-by-jowl and defying any classification of the street as a whole. On the other hand, housing for the new industrial working class covered huge areas with monotonous, mean, nondescript buildings, with sometimes bands of coloured brick, or strips of mass-produced machine carving, pathetically endeavouring to give character and romance to the basic box. Of the last, Ewart Johns writes, 'The great mass of streets of hideous terraces which still make up much of Salford, and other parts of the Manchester conurbation, are hard to reconcile with any idea of a sense of design, but it is possible to see, if we can temporarily suspend our faculties of criticising the inhumanity of the present condition of these places, the almost despairing attempt to raise the roofs into a Gothic pitch, and to point the chimneys skyward . . .' A vertical version of this horizontal squalor is the tenement block.

There were, it is true, contemporary calls for a 'new' style, but they had little effect, for, as Scott wrote 'All we at present know is that our opponents have decided that we are wrong, but this discussion will produce only perplexity unless they tell us clearly and specifically what is right. When we ask for the practical working out of what our opponents are so fond of urging, the result is absolutely nil.'

It follows, therefore, that the term 'Victorian' is adequate as a label for a period, but not for a style. I suggest that for style we shall have to be content with 'neo' labels, and where diversity prevents us from putting a street or area under one class, we shall have to be content with 'mixed'. For the 'salubrious dwellings for the working poor' we could use the phrase 'By-law Building', as most of the surviving examples were built under by-laws stemming from the Public Health Act of 1875; but this does not apply to the earlier part of the reign, and can also refer to quite good, substantial housing. I would therefore suggest *Victorian Utility* for the meaner sort (VU could well be Victorian Ugly!), and for the better-built, larger, middle-class, terrace housing, usually with bay windows, gables, and a small front garden, I would use the term *Victorian Terrace.*

Edwardian 1901–1918

Edward VII died in 1910, but the Edwardian period is often extended to include the years up to the First World War, and here is taken to include the War as very little building took place during it. The term should not be confused with 'Edwardian' referring to Edward I and castle building.

This was a time of 'Pomp and Circumstance' in public buildings, still using old styles but favouring the Baroque freedom. It was characterised by variety, exuberance, decoration, curved gables, and deep rustication, mockingly called the "Wrenaissance' style. A popular form, seen in many Public Libraries, was in red brick with heavy white stone quoins, white cupolas, and curved gables. Very characteristic are large windows with semi-circular heads.

Domestic architecture, on the other hand, was tending basically towards an unfussy Gothic style, and respect for good materials meant that some very sound building was done, particularly in the more expensive suburban houses. Some attempt at slum clearance was started and simple blocks of flats began to appear. These were to house the poor; the middle-class aim was no longer for a town-house but for a suburban 'cottage' in its own patch of ground. The simplicity of the Georgian style was once again beginning to attract.

This period saw the start of the Garden Suburb. Out of reaction to the sprawling, choking, Victorian city came a work of enormous influence, Ebenezer Howard's *Tomorrow,* published in 1898 and republished in 1902 as *Garden Cities of Tomorrow.* It advocated low-density, open-planned towns of 30 000 inhabitants with their own industries and surrounded by Green Belts. They were Cities *in* Gardens rather than *of* Gardens, but the low density did, of course, mean that there would be plenty of private garden space. Howard himself founded two Garden Cities, Letchworth in 1903 and Welwyn in 1919 (taken over in 1948 as the nucleus of a New Town). His ideas led to the 1946 New Towns Act and the official Green Belt policy of 1953.

The idea of the Garden City was also influential in a way its author did not intend. One aspect only, that of low-density housing with ample garden space, was seized on and led to a pattern of 'Garden Suburbs' (e.g. Hampstead Garden Suburb, 1907), and a debased houses-in-open-space style which is the basis of a great deal of 'housing estate' design in this country. In 1918 the Tudor Walters Report of the Committee on the Housing of the Working Classes recommended 12 houses to the acre (Letchworth was designed for 10, and 15 was recommended for the New Towns), and this number has become something of a sacred object to town planners.

The low density is mentioned here because, although it is mainly a matter of layout, it has affected our building styles, mainly by eliminating long terraces, so that by far the most common type of house built since 1918 is the two- or three-bedroomed semi-detached. The idea has also worked in the opposite direction since 1945, influenced by Le Corbusier's 'Ville Radieuse', in the provision of open space by piling dwellings on top of each other in the form of flats. Thus we have two basic types of twentieth-century dwellings, the matchbox and the shoe-box, and the latter may lie on its side, as a slab, or on its end, as a tower.

Inter-war 1919–1939

Housing was now normally in estates, including the housing financed for the first time by local authorities, and in 'ribbon development' along roads. Terraces were not favoured and the majority of houses were detached or semi-detached. Bungalows were becoming popular. In Council estates the styles tended to be uniform and plain; in the private ones there was a somewhat pathetic attempt to give individuality to different houses. This produced a style which has been called 'Builder's All-sorts' and which is basically what I shall call 'Romantic', tending to reflect, in poor materials, a medieval style, although neo-Georgian was beginning to come into favour as well.

Neo-Georgian, mostly plain-walled in brick, with white woodwork round regularly-placed windows, and with timid pediments, became increasingly favoured for public buildings such as post offices and town halls.

Perhaps the biggest change in detail was the introduction of metal-framed casement windows. Building material was still mainly brick or stone, but reinforced concrete was becoming fashionable and might be used in larger buildings, such as blocks of flats (including the new 'luxury' flats), hotels, or shopping streets. Unfortunately the techniques of handling concrete were often not well understood and some of the work in this material has stained and cracked badly. This is often the case, too, where an imitation concrete surface has been put over brick.

The so-called 'International Modern' style did not affect the general pattern of building in Britain. Where it occurs it can be distinguished by smooth white walls, cubic forms with flat roofs, long lines of windows often taken round corners, and concrete balconies.

There are no generally agreed type-labels. *International Modern* is probably the most generally accepted, but Walter Gropius to whom the style is often attributed strongly denied that there was any such thing. 'Builder's All-sorts' is not a respectable label, and for the average sort of inter-war, and indeed post-war, house, with a front gable, a bay window, a recessed porch, and brick walls covered in pebble-dash, I would suggest the term *Romantic*, not so much for the result as for the intention. The plainer, flat-fronted house, with possibly a porch, and probably a saddle-back roof rising from the level top of the front and back walls (an eaves house), often found on Council estates, has been referred to as 'Classical'. This term, however, has associations with pillars and pediments, and I prefer to coin the term *Rectilinear*.

As we shall see, modern high buildings are also Rectilinear, so we may perhaps call the house type 'Rectilinear Low'. Similarly, the Romantic can appear in a number of weak imitations of old styles, so we may add the prefix 'mock-' (which is preferable to 'neo-'; e.g. mock-Tudor.

Post-war—after 1945

Since 1945, apart from the 'pre-fab', which might have marked a break-through in building construction and did not, small houses have tended to look much as between the wars, with perhaps a tendency to a greater proportion of Rectilinear types, sometimes seeking effect not by decoration but by a variety of colour or texture panels. The terrace has come back into favour to a certain extent, but low-density housing is still the main pattern.

The new element in the townscape is the high block, mostly steel-framed, with great expanses of glass. Mostly the blocks are 'high-rise' or 'point block' flats or offices and they rise either out of landscaped greenery or from a sea of low buildings. Unlike most British inter-war steel-frame buildings they do not disguise their construction behind apparently massive walls, but by using thin cladding give an impression of lightness, especially when supported on legs (*pilotis*). This relationship of external form to internal structure can, however, give a 'boxiness' to the building which is often criticised. Reinforced concrete allows for a freer, more flowing shape and can produce almost Baroque form, but is less common and is rarely used with great imagination.

There is no standard term for the tall boxes. I suggest *Rectilinear high*, or possibly *Grid high*.

REFERENCES

Banister Fletcher, *A History of Architecture on the Comparative Method*, 17th edn., revised R. A. Cordingley, Athlone Press, 1961.

This large, expensive, well-known book may be arranged on the basis of theories not everywhere accepted today, but as a source of fact and particularly of illustration it is invaluable.

Brunskill, R. W., *Vernacular Architecture*, Faber, 1970.

Very good on materials and structure of small buildings.

Iredale, D., *This Old House*, Shire Publications, 1968.

An inexpensive pocket-guide to sources for dating houses and tracing their history. Well written and illustrated, it is practical and useful.

Kidson, P. and P. Murray, *A History of English Architecture*, Penguin, 1965.

Like most histories of architecture, this tends to concentrate on 'important' buildings, but gives background information necessary for a study of your town.

Lancaster, O., *Pillar to Post*, Murray, 1963 (first published 1938).

Brilliantly satirical drawings of the major phases in English architecture, with a brief text which makes many interesting points.

Penoyre, J. and H. Ryan, *The Observer's Book of Architecture*, Warne, 1958.

An excellent introduction, with very helpful drawings.

Richards, J. M., *The Functional Tradition,* Architectural Press, 1958.

Dealing with early industrial buildings, this is largely a picture book, but the comments are illuminating.

Richards, J. M., *An Introduction to Modern Architecture*, rev. edn., Penguin, 1962.

Concerned with individual buildings rather than towns, this book is not only an excellent introduction to modern methods and ideas but also has a good bibliography.

Summerson, J., *Georgian London*, Penguin, 1962.

A fascinating book, useful both for accounts of Georgian style, where the drawings are particularly helpful, and for the history of the influences behind development.

West, T., *The History of Architecture in England*, U.L.P., 1963.

An excellent introduction to the subject. Good line drawings, and lists of typical buildings.

ARCHITECTURAL VOCABULARY

In writing about townscapes it is useful to have a certain amount of technical vocabulary at your command. This can be achieved by studying books on architecture, but as a starter some of the basic architectural terms are illustrated in the following pages. For further information you could consult:

Earnshaw, W., *Discovering Houses*, U.L.P., 1959.

Although written for children, this book contains a great deal of useful detail and is well illustrated.

Fleming, J. (ed.), *The Penguin Dictionary of Architecture*, Penguin, 1966.

The difficulty with using a dictionary such as this, is that if you do not know the name of a thing, you cannot look it up. Illustrations are therefore important, though the size of this book does not of course permit lavishness in this respect.

Osborne, A. L., *A Dictionary of English Domestic Architecture*, Country Life, 1954.

As the name indicates, this covers a narrower field than the above, and there is more room for illustrations, which are good.

ROOFS

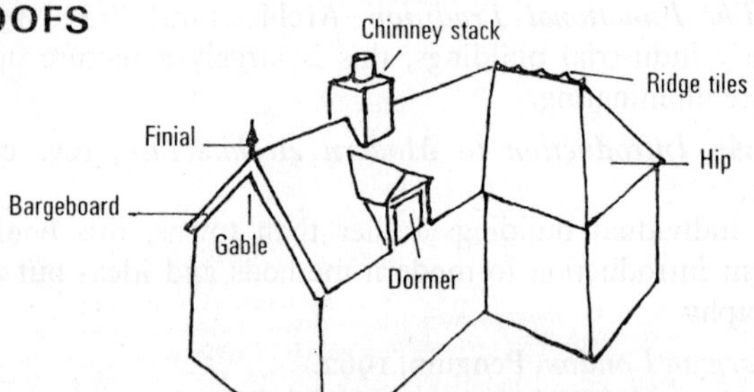

Mansard roof

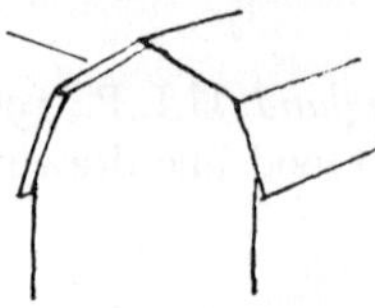

Gabled or saddleback roof

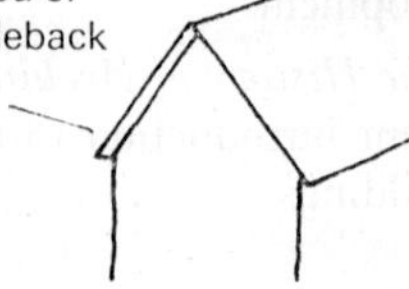

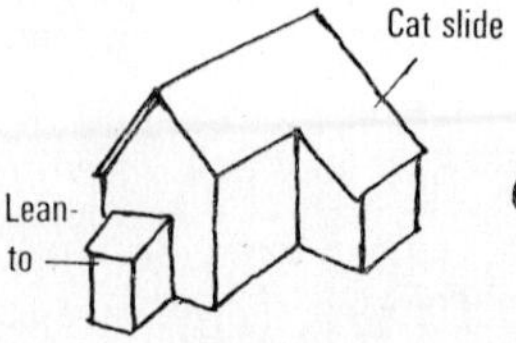

Dutch gable

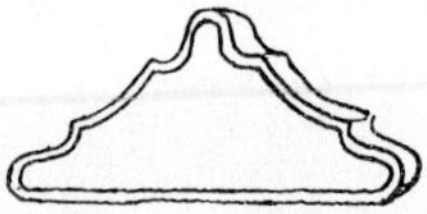

Stepped gable

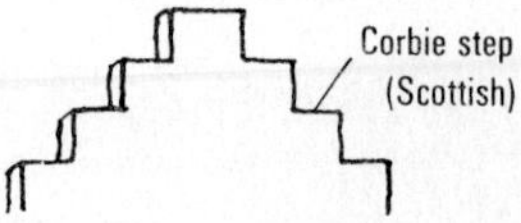

Tiles

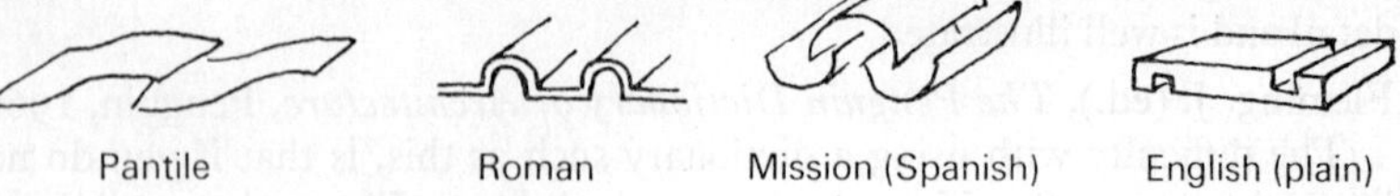

Battlements or crenellation

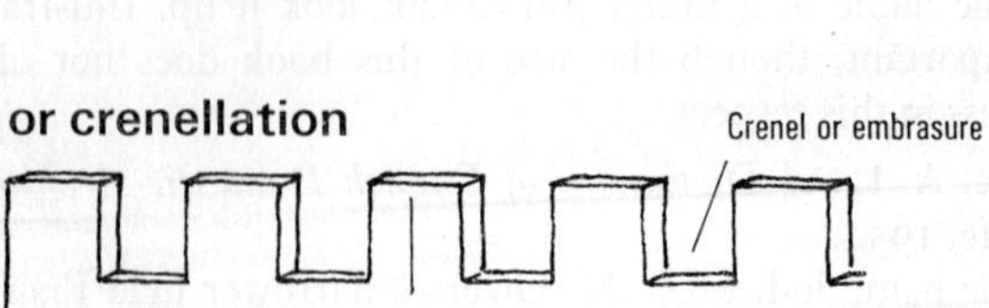

WALLS

Stone

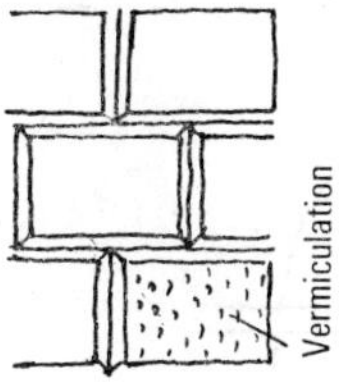

Rustication

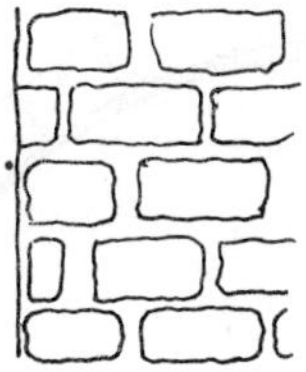

Coursed rubble

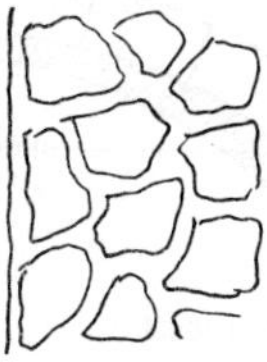

Random rubble

Ashlar

Brick

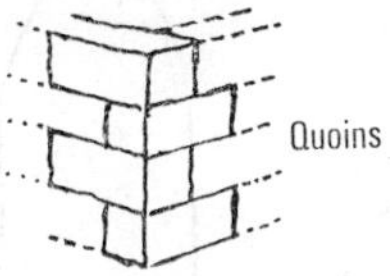

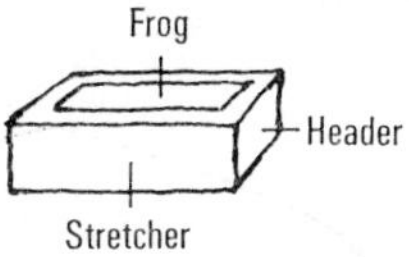

Standard brick (pre-metric)

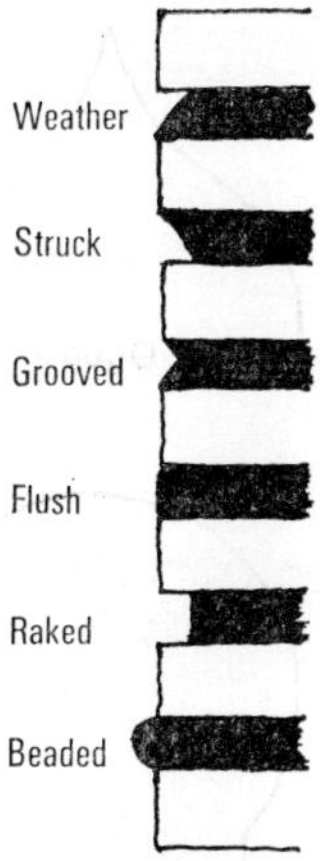

Mortar joints

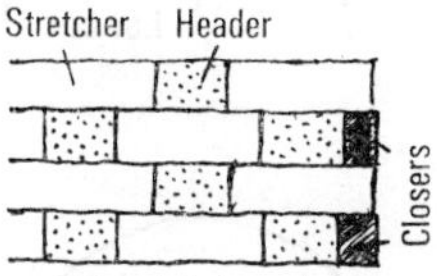

Flemish bond

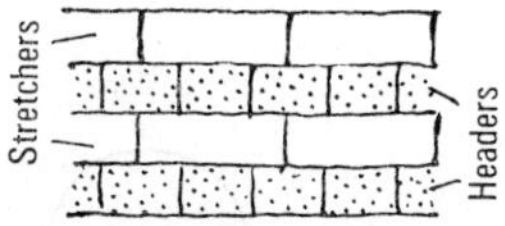

English bond

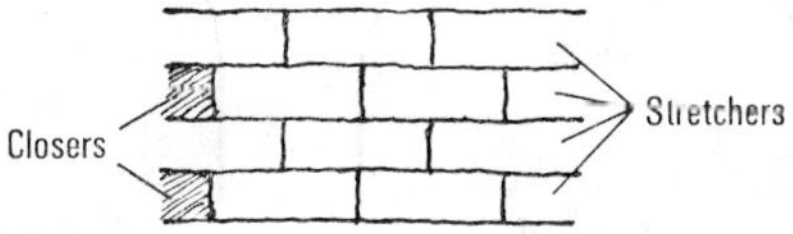

Stretcher bond

Others

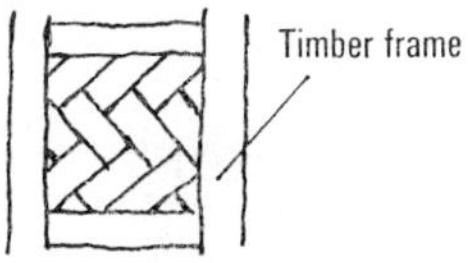

Brick nogging

Weatherboard (clapboard)

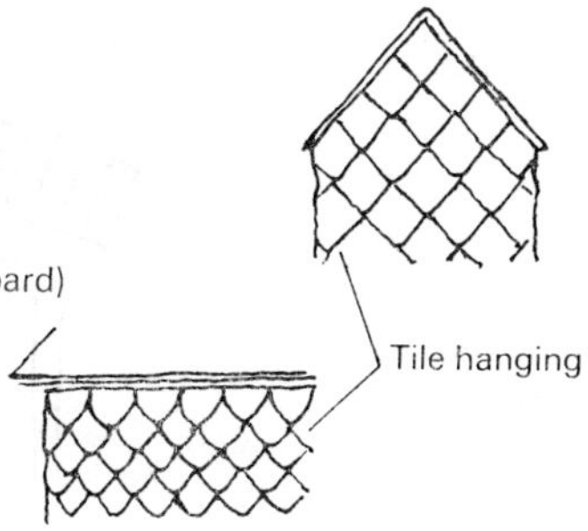

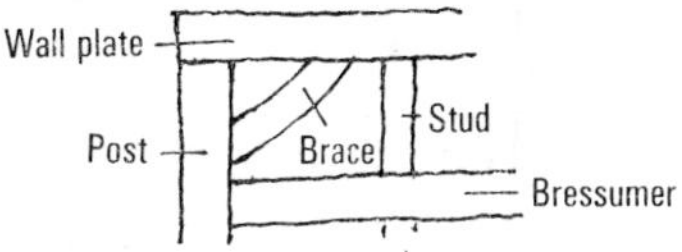

Timber framing

ARCHES

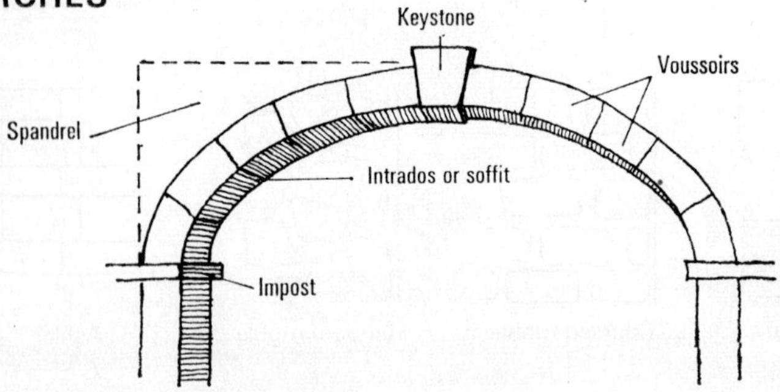
Keystone
Voussoirs
Spandrel
Intrados or soffit
Impost

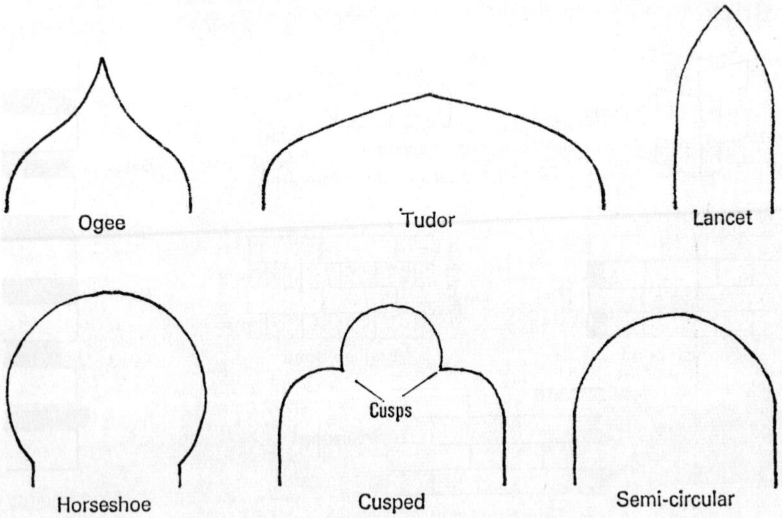
Ogee
Tudor
Lancet
Horseshoe
Cusps
Cusped
Semi-circular

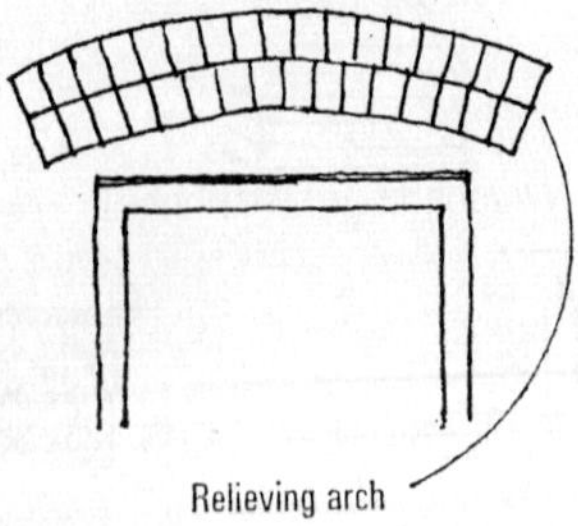
Relieving arch

PILLARS

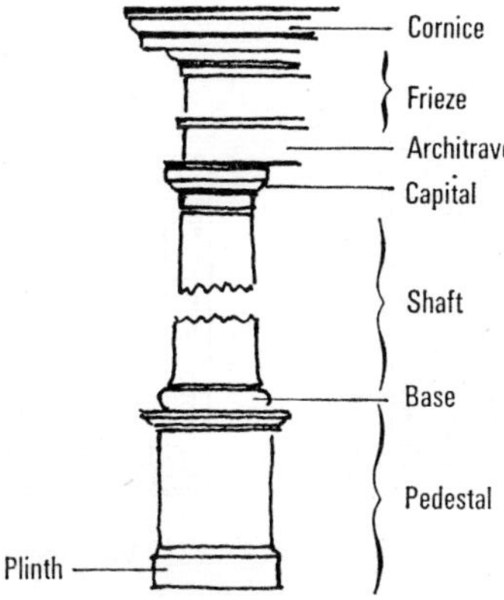

Classical capitals

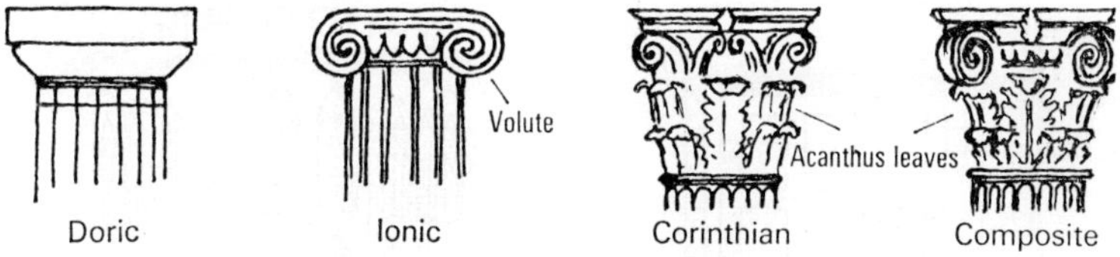

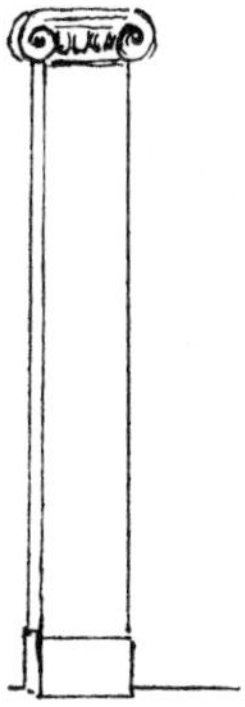
Pilaster

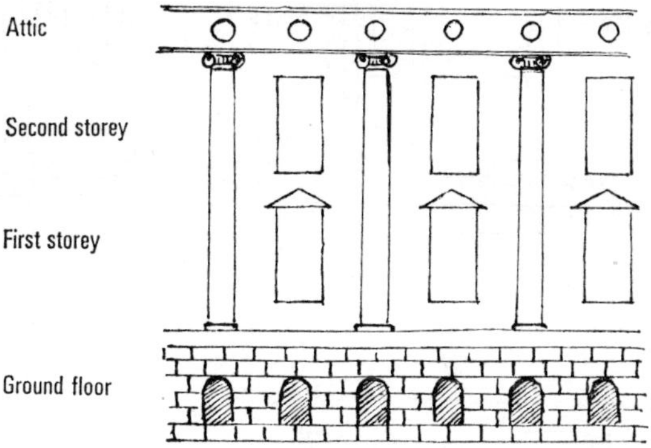

Giant columns

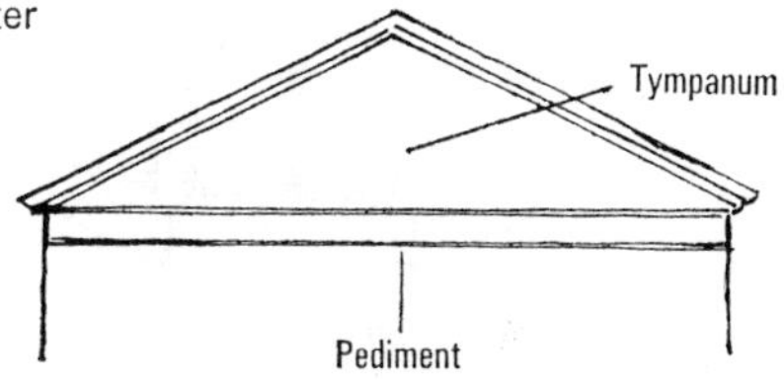

WINDOWS

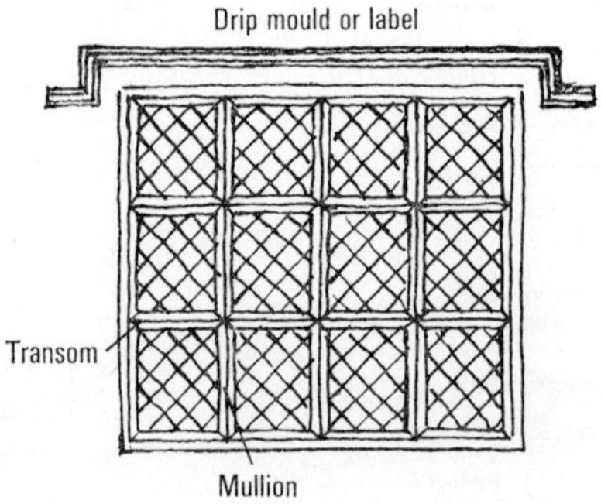

Mediaeval window

Venetian window

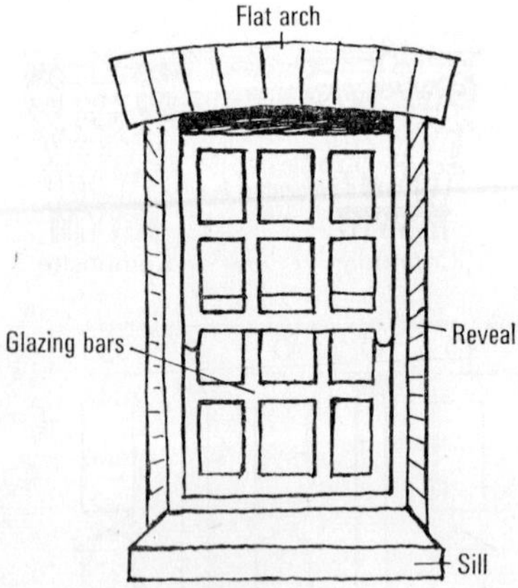

Sash window

Oriel window

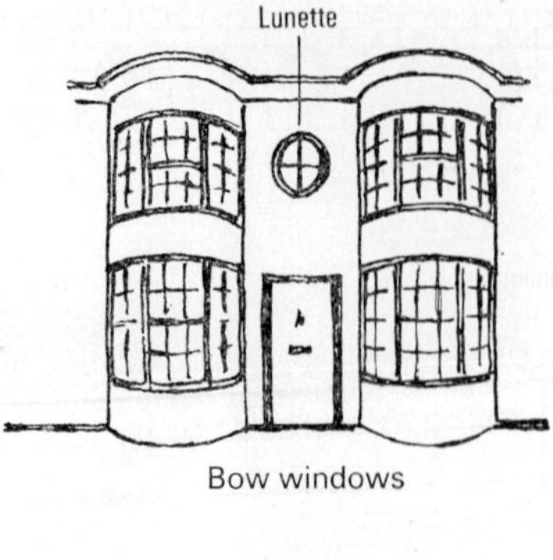

Bow windows

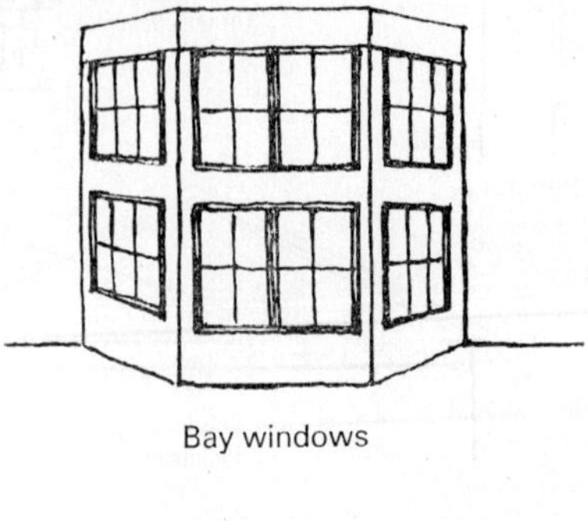

Bay windows

DOORS

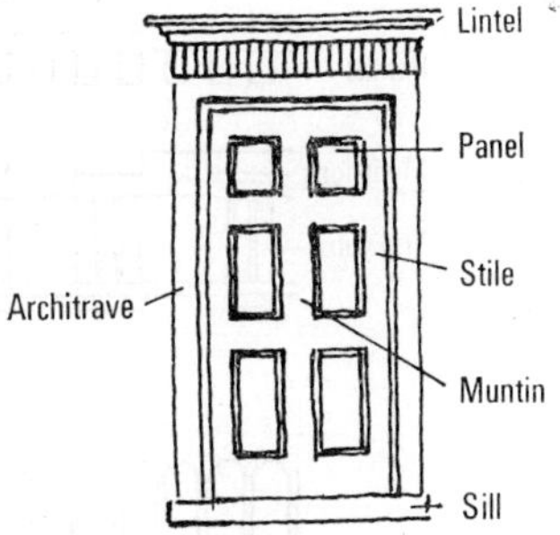

Fanlight

Pediment (or overdoor)

Portico

Shell canopy

Segmental pediment

Open pediment

Broken pediment

Scroll pediment

Broken segmental pediment

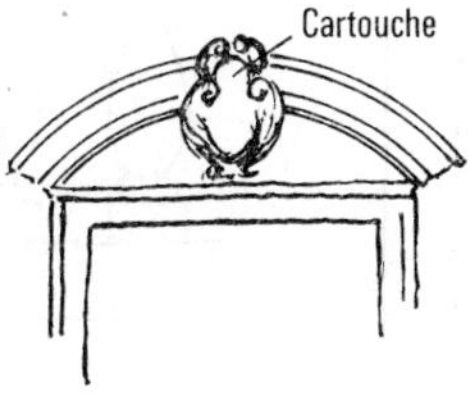

Console or bracket

DECORATION

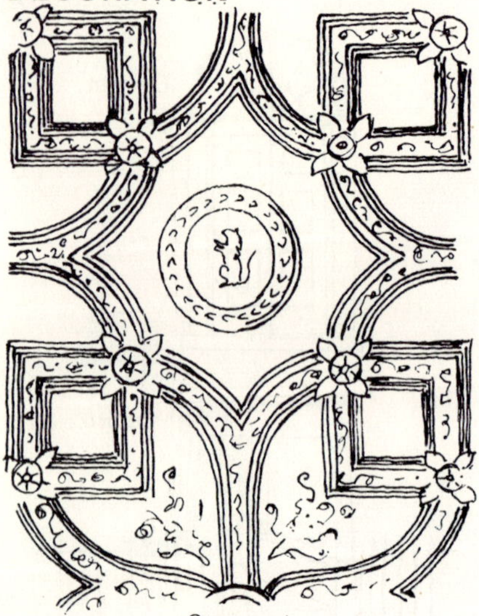

Strapwork

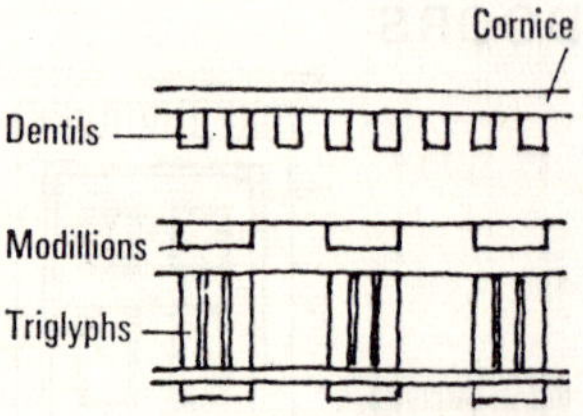

Fluting

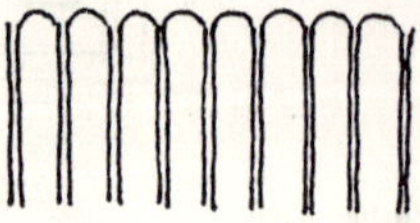

Festoon (swag)

Patera

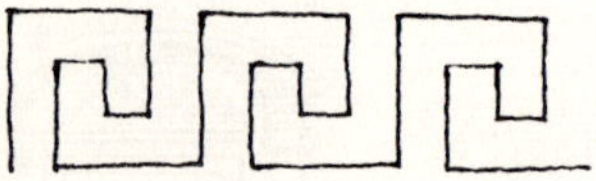

Greek fret (key)

Running dog (Vitruvian scroll)

Egg and dart

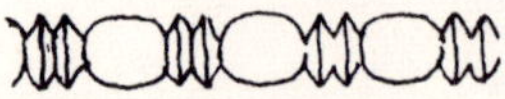

Bead and reel

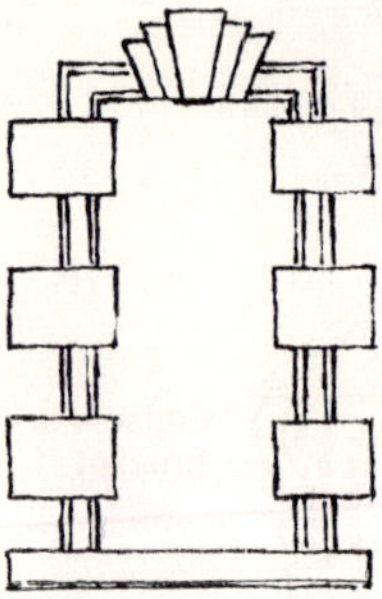

Gibbs surround

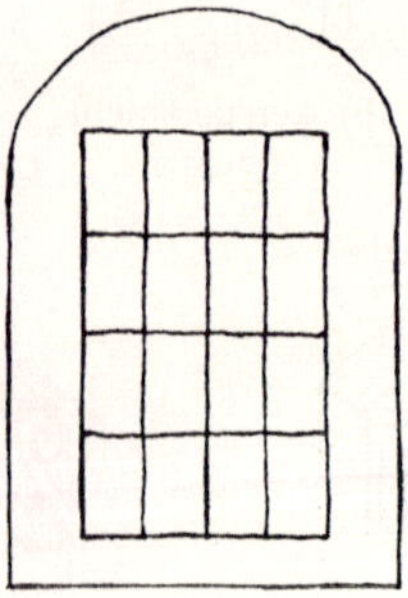

Depressed arch

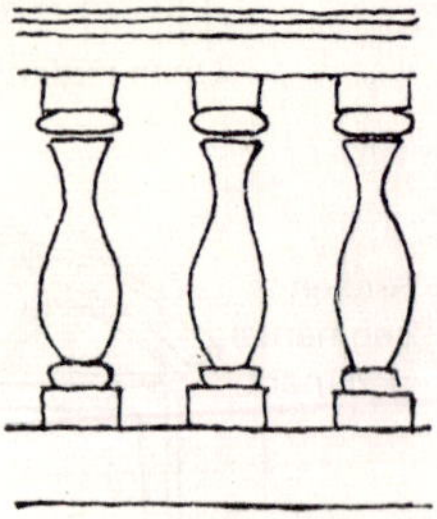

Balustrade

Townscape survey

Maps of geographical features, functional zones, and the distribution of different building materials and styles, will tell us a good deal about the appearance of the town, especially if they are supplemented by photographs and sketches, but they will still fail to give an overall impression of stretches of townscape. To a large extent this impression will have to be conveyed in words, but it is also worthwhile to attempt a condensed analytical expression in map form.

The following method, although still experimental, is one which I have found useful. It is based on looking at a whole stretch of street, asking oneself questions about its visual characteristics, and entering the answers in code on a recording sheet. At present I am using eleven questions, and therefore the sheet needs eleven columns. The questions, together with coded answers, are as follows:

1) Is it unbroken (ignoring small passages), or in blocks? (T, for terrace, or B)
2) Is it flat-faced, or broken by bays and other protuberances? (FF or BF)
3) Is the skyline generally even, or is it broken or fretted by gables, pinnacles, towers, etc.? (ES or BS)
4) Is the architectural style generally the same throughout, or is it varied? (AS or AV)
5) Are the surfaces of the buildings generally plain, or are they highly ornamented? (FP or FO)
6) What is the usual number of storeys? (Write in the number)
7) What is the predominant architectural style? (e.g. the code on page 50)
8) What is the predominant building material? (e.g. the code on page 51)
9) What is the predominant colour? (Use name or appropriate initial)
10) Are there front gardens, or areas, or none? (FG, A, or X)
11) Is the street wide, medium, or narrow? (SW, SM, or SN)

The following are actual examples:

A Georgian terrace—T/FF/ES/AS/FP/3/G/S/Grey/X/SM
A Victorian terrace T/BF/BS/AV/FO/3/V/B/Red/FG/SM
An inter-war ribbon development—B/BF/ES/AS/FP/2/I/B/Red/FG/SW

Sometimes the two sides of a street built at different times will have to be recorded separately; in others one street may have to be divided into separate stretches. Particular difficulty is found where the street shows a great mixture of styles. We have then got to decide whether one is dominant in giving character to the street, whether we should enter several styles under 7), or whether we should simply enter AM for 'Mixed'.

When it comes to mapping the information it might appear that the number of possible combinations would call for an impossible number of symbols, but in most cases the street types tend to fall into a few groups, and much of the difficulty can be met by using inter-related symbols:

	T/FF/ES	The long block shows it is a terrace; the even sides show that there are neither bays nor gables; the clear interior shows that the architectural style is consistent.
	T/FF/BS/AS	Gables added
	T/BF/BS/AS/BF	Bays added
	B/FF/ES	The blocks which show that this is not a terrace are arranged conventionally and do not indicate actual buildings.
	T/FF/ES/AV	Divisions show that the architecture is varied.

Colour can be added by using a colour wash. Number of storeys, building material and architectural period can be shown by adding letters or numbers, if the scale of the map allows, or may be drawn on a separate map or overlay.

A similar idea for recording is outlined by E. Raisz in his *Principles of Cartography* (McGraw Hill, 1962). He has invented the term *geostenography* for a rapid survey from car, bus or even aeroplane. The observer works up the page of a notebook, right and left of a centre line, noting mileage, altitude and direction, and entering details in 'geostenograms' of which the standard model for buildings is:

Width

Height *or* storeys — TYPE — Value (I-IV) / Age (*years*) / Material

Base

(*can be basement or ground floor*)

Victorian Renaissance. Lloyds Bank, Corn Street, Bristol. A highly decorated version of what has been called the 'bracket-and-mantelshelf' style. The lower columns are Doric, the upper are Ionic.

Victorian Gothic villa. Cumberland Road, Bristol. Note the gables with decorated bargeboards, the stone mullions, drip mouldings, and castellated porch. On the ground floor are bay windows with oriels above.

Edwardian Baroque. Shop in Oxford Street, London. The use of white Portland stone and red brick is very characteristic of this period; so is the lavish use of ornament. There is less carving than on the Victorian bank on the previous page, but it is much bolder and more bulging.

Modern rectilinear style. Monmouth House, Cwmbran New Town. Here the architect has tried to give visual appeal by a repeating pattern of rectangular shapes, texture and colour, and by horizontal bands of modelling on the concrete surface of the major slab. The skyline is broken by what look like broad battlements. Do you think this is visually a success?

Thus a one-year-old, first-class, four-storey apartment block, in brick, would be

I
IV Ap 1y
br

This type of recording by arranging figures or symbols in a pre-arranged sequence around a centre is, of course, similar to that used in weather maps. It can be adapted to show any desired combination of characteristics, limited only by the space available.

REFERENCE

Cullen, G., *Townscape*, Architectural Press, 1961.

To Cullen the study of Townscape is an exercise in aesthetics and the means by which town planning can ensure visual pleasure. Townscaping is to him an art to be applied to the design of cities. His detailed analysis of actual townscapes should be carefully studied and will help our understanding and judgement.

New building

A good deal of what we have to say about the forces which determined the siting of buildings in the past must be conjecture, but for buildings which are now going up we can investigate these factors at first hand; moreover they will be a guide to future development. It is therefore useful to plot on a town map any building in progress, and to note all the details about it as we would for any already in existence. By contacting the people responsible, it is then possible to report on why the particular building style and materials were used. The map could also show any road developments in progress. A series of such maps over the years would be of great use to future students of the town.

Quality of buildings

This can relate to architectural and/or historical interest, the state of the fabric, or the building's monetary value.

(i) *Architectural and/or historical interest*

There is an official list of buildings so scheduled by the Ministry of Housing and Local Government which can probably be consulted at the local library or at Council offices. Such 'listed' buildings cannot be legally demolished or altered with ease. This helps to preserve them but there is a danger that they may become 'fossilised' in an alien environment of new building. You may well wish to add to the list.

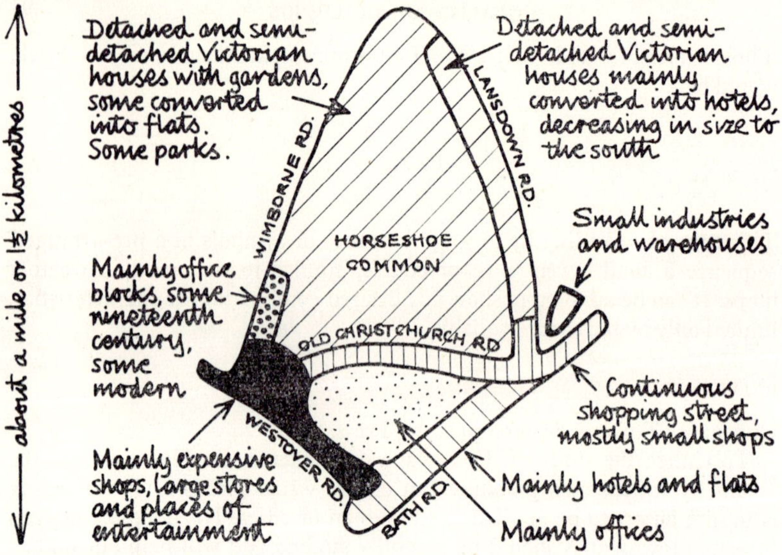

Figure 18a Land use: part of Bournemouth. Data from a day's rapid survey.

It would be interesting to make a survey of buildings and streets from the point of view of their architectural quality, classifying them as Outstanding, Very Good, Good, and Poor. It is difficult to say how an absolute standard of judgement for this can be found, and in this Age of Uncertainty there is a lack of generally accepted convention which, although in many ways healthy, tends to lead to confusion. It is easier to make a judgement on the convenience of a building, or on area layout* than on its visual quality. There is no room to discuss this here, and all I can recommend is that you read and observe as widely as possible, make your decisions, and try to produce reasons for them.

(ii) *The state of the fabric*

Although there may well be hidden defects, you can at least make a map of buildings that are outwardly in a state of decay, and this adds another feature to the total townscape picture. It is also useful to know where the main areas of decayed buildings are located, and to attempt an explanation. This study of decay is linked with the study of weathering (*see pages* 43–45). Some information may be obtained from the Building Inspector's Department of the local Council.

* An interesting discussion of this will be found in Chermayeff, S. and C. Alexander, *Community and Privacy: Towards a New Architecture of Humanism*, Penguin, 1966.

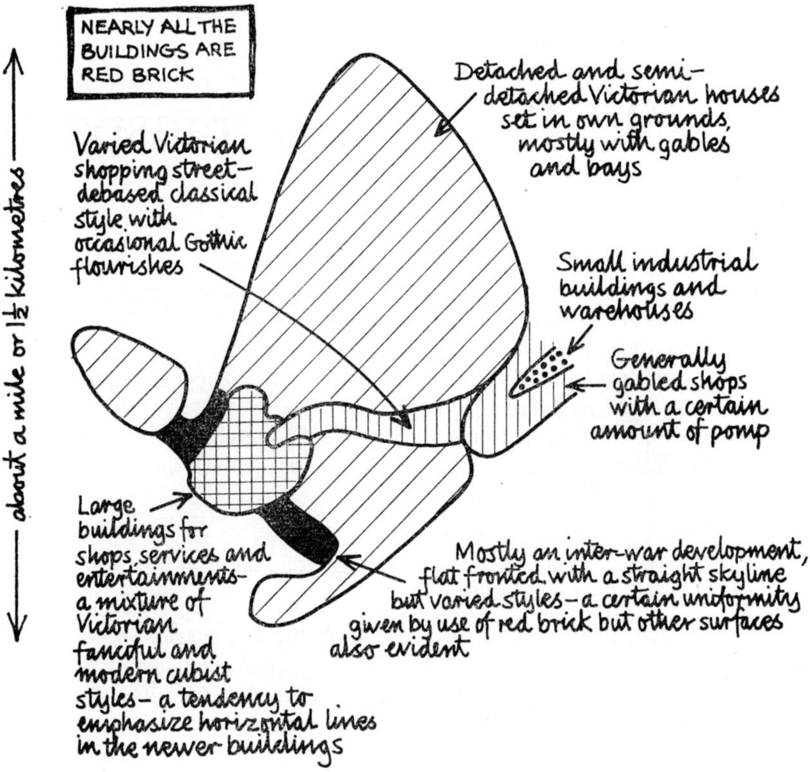

Figure 18b Townscapes: part of Bournemouth. Data from a day's rapid survey.

(iii) *Monetary value*

Some idea of the market value of buildings in different parts of the town can be obtained from agents' notices, and this can be compared with past prices obtained from a study of old newspapers. Although changes in the value of money make a comparison of prices difficult, we can at least get some idea of relative changes between the same areas at different times. We may find, for example, that although all prices have risen in the last hundred years, they have risen much more rapidly in some areas than in others, and in some cases what were relatively high-price areas have become relatively low-price ones; from this we can see something of the changing location of 'fashionable' areas.

Another approach is to study the rateable value of property as shown in the Council's rating register.

9. Streets and transport

Street patterns

In studying a town it is often impossible to 'see the streets for the houses'. By tracing off the streets as thick black lines a pattern may emerge which may not have been evident before, and we may be able to divide the town into street-pattern regions such as *small-mesh grid*, *wide-mesh grid*, *concentric*, *radial*, *spider's web* (a combination of concentric and radial), and *amorphous* (lacking a definite pattern).

Explanation of these patterns can be sought in terms of topography, and in the history of the growth of the town, particularly in relation to:

(*a*) land holdings
(*b*) changing architectural fashion
(*c*) changing regional function (as, for example, the arrival of a railway, or developments in industry)

It must be remembered that there have probably been periods when new patterns were superimposed on the old, or followed the demolition or destruction by fire or enemy action of an older pattern, although after destruction the power of property rights may have prevented any drastic alteration.

The names of street, as we have seen, may give clues to their past history—e.g. Cheap (market), Westgate, Castle, Strand, Milk, Barton (barley-place or farm), Station—but we must remember that streets may have been re-named, and also that the name may have become distorted with the passage of time.

Some street patterns may have been deliberately planned, as in the case of modern estates, some medieval foundations such as Salisbury or Hull,* and eighteenth-century Edinburgh or nineteenth-century Newcastle. In many cases, however, they grew up around ancient ownership plots and developed in a fashion that appears haphazard until related to these old holdings, as has been done by M. R. G. Conzen in his study of Alnwick (Northumberland).†

Interesting leads to the study of streets are given by W. G. Hoskins in *Local History in England* (Longman, 1959) and A. E. Smailes in *The Geography of Towns* (Hutchinson University Library, rev. edn., 1966).

* See Beresford, M. W., *New Towns of the Middle Ages*, Lutterworth Press, 1967.

† *Transactions of the Institute of British Geographers*, No. 27, 1960.

Illuminating as an analysis of a town in terms of its ground plan may be, it must be stressed that this is an incomplete way of approaching urban geography and can only be a part of a more comprehensive study.

Traffic studies

Traffic, both vehicular and pedestrian, is a noticeable feature of the urban landscape. A town survey would be sadly lacking if no reference were made to this important element. Unfortunately a full set of figures, covering all aspects, is difficult to compile and would involve questioning many drivers and pedestrians—and only the police have a legal right to stop traffic. Useful work on traffic flow, however, can be done by observation.

For a general introduction and a particular point of view, see the 'Buchanan Report', *Traffic in Towns* (H.M.S.O., 1963). For details of method, consult *Research on Road Traffic* (Road Research Laboratory, H.M.S.O., 1965).

Traffic flow

The flow of traffic can be measured at a point, during a given period, by counting vehicles as they pass. Naturally the flow, and its density in terms of direction, will vary with the day of the week, the season, and the time of day, so that counts at different times will have to be made. These can be selected after an investigation into the times of maximum and minimum flow. From the point of view of road planning, it is of course the maximum which is more important, and you may prefer to concentrate on this. For observing traffic in both directions it is a great help to have a partner, and even with uni-directional traffic the work is easier if divided between an observer and a booker. Alternatively, it may be possible for the observer to record the information on a tape-recorder and transcribe it later at home—providing that the recorder does not go wrong.

Some kind of classification should be used, and a form drawn up to make recording easier. The following classification is used by the Ministry of Transport:

Pedal cycles
Solo motor cycles
Motor cycle combinations
Mopeds (cycles with motors and pedals)
Scooters (motor cycles with small wheels)
Cars and taxis (including light three-wheeled cars, invalid carriages, cars with trailers, and dual-purpose vehicles appearing to be used as cars)
Buses and coaches (including works' buses)

Light vans (all commercial vehicles of less than 30 cwt. unladen weight, pedestrian controlled vehicles, such as hand-pulled electric milk floats, and dual-purpose vehicles appearing to be used for commercial purposes)
Other vehicles (including all heavy commercial vehicles, tractors, and traction engines. Unusual traffic such as steam-rollers, hand barrows, animals, and horse-drawn vehicles are not included)

A somewhat shorter list was used in the Oxford survey of 1957:

Scooters and motor cycles
Cars, taxis and motor cycle combinations
Private coaches and buses
Service buses
Light commercial vehicles
Heavy commercial vehicles

Town...................... Street, place..............

Date...................... Weather....................

Direction................. State of road..............

Recorder.................. Time.......................

Sheet No..................

	1	2	3	4	5	6	7	8	9	10	(up to 30)	Total
Pedal cycles	/	/	/	/								
Solo m/c	/	/										
(etc.)												

Figure 19 A typical traffic-flow recording sheet
The various classes of vehicle are listed in the left-hand column, allowing a reasonable number of horizontal lines for each. For each vehicle an oblique stroke is entered in the next vacant column. It should be possible to record up to 1,000 vehicles per hour.

Public services

The flow of public service vehicles, including trains, can be found from a study of timetables. Here again there will be variations at different times and seasons. An important factor is accessibility of public transport; this can be worked out on a map by drawing *isochrones* (lines of equal time) enclosing all places that can be reached in a given length of time, usually half-an-hour's walk at 3 m.p.h., from a bus stop or a station. It is important that these should represent real journeys by men walking, not by crows flying. An isochrone is not therefore necessarily parallel to a bus route, or in a circle round a station.

The number of buses, or indeed of any vehicles, along a route can be shown in a *flow map*, where the frequency is related to the width to which the route is drawn. Inward and outward journeys can be distinguished by using two colours. A simpler method is to show the route as a set of parallel lines, the number of lines corresponding to the frequency with which vehicles pass along it.

Destination and purpose

It is important to know how many vehicles use a route but is is also of value, particularly in planning, to know *why* the route is being used and how frequently. The most accurate way is to stop a sample selection of cars out of a traffic stream and question the occupants, but this calls for police participation. A simpler method is to have observers at all points of entry and exit who note down the registration numbers of cars and the times that they are seen. It is thus possible to sort out the following categories:

(*a*) Cars passing through the town
(*b*) Cars making a short stay in town
(*c*) Cars making a long stay in town
(*d*) Cars starting from town (that is, traffic generated by the town)

The normal period of observation is from 6 a.m. to 10 p.m. but it is sometimes confined to peak hours. Sampling can be done by recording only those vehicles whose numbers end in one or more specified digits.

This sort of recording obviously calls for a team of observers, but in a small town with limited access points you might be able to organise this. It would be useful not only from the point of view of studying traffic but also in giving guidance about the relationship of the town to its region.

Parking

There are two main factors here—general distribution of parked cars, and duration of stay. Recording the former is easy—if rather boring—and consists of walking round a route and marking, either in a notebook or on a street map, the number and types of vehicles parked. This should be done at peak periods. You can then work out a *parking index*, which is the number of cars actually standing at a kerb expressed as a percentage of the number of 6-metre (20-foot) lengths along the kerb. Any detail of parking restrictions should also be noted. Duration of stay will involve recording car numbers and re-visiting at fixed intervals of, say, half-an-hour. It is only necessary to record the last three digits of the car number. There may be a possibility of enlisting the help of Traffic Wardens.

Problem spots

In any town there are places which present a particularly difficult problem to traffic flow and these merit attention and discussion.

Pedestrians

Flow can be measured as for vehicles, although crowd density may make the task more difficult. On the other hand it is much easier to observe the route taken by a pedestrian than by a vehicle. The difficulty is to decide which pedestrian to observe, and therefore some form of sampling must be used. The easiest is to select the *n*th person who passes a certain point or emergers from a certain place, such as a bus.

To find out how many people are in a crowded street is not easy as there are always people entering and leaving, and the people present are mostly moving about. A method which gives a good approximation is called the 'moving observer method'. In this the observer walks from one end of the street, or section of the street, to the other and then back again, keeping the same steady pace. He notes the number of people he passes on each trip, whichever direction they are moving, and *subtracts* the people who overtake him. He need not do the arithmetic on the spot, but simply record plus and minus. The average of the two trips gives a good approximation of the total number of people in the street.

External transport patterns

Railways

An event of fundamental importance in the development of many towns was the coming of the railway in the nineteenth century. Because of high land values and dense building in the centre of the town, and the vested interests in property there, the line rarely penetrated the heart of the town and the mainline stations tended to be off-centre. This often meant that a burst of building development, often industrial, could take place in the vicinity of the railway. It also meant that labour and raw materials could flow in at a far greater and far cheaper rate than before, and it extended the market range for the products. This had a particular value for inland centres.

A further result was that when a town offered not goods but special facilities such as a sandy beach, a good shopping centre or a fine theatre, the market it could draw on was tremendously increased. It also meant that the greater ease and cheapness of travel acquainted provincial people with the features of the metropolis and so provoked emulation, while the railway hotels set a new standard of provincial catering.

Railway historians have been busy and there are many books dealing with this subject, notably the various volumes of *The Regional History of the Railways of Great Britain*, edited by D. St. J. Thomas and published by David and Charles.

Canals

In some areas—notably the Midlands—canals are still an important form of transport, and although the canal age was brought rapidly to a close by the coming of the railways, canals still feature in many towns, even if they may now be little more than weedy depressions, with broken locks and decaying pumping stations, wharfs and inns. Even more than in the case of the railway, their course is closely related to relief.

For canals we can consult the many books by C. Hadfield and by L. T. C. Rolt. Some information about both railways and waterways can be obtained from the British Transport Archives, and maps and plans may also be held in the County Record Office.

Roads

Main roads affect the geography of a town in relation to the accessibility they provide to and from the surrounding region, and in the volume of through traffic which they carry. If we have conducted, or have access to, a traffic survey, we shall have important information about this, but an understanding of the actual path of the roads involves a study both of local topography and history.

The first major development in road-making and improvement after the Roman era came in the eighteenth century with the formation of Turnpike Trusts. Information about these can be found in old maps, Parish records and Council minutes, and in the records of the Trusts themselves, probably available in the local Record Office. Some Trusts were inefficient, but many made considerable improvements to the 'line' of the road, widening, straightening, and improving gradients, so that many features of present-day main roads are due to their activities.

When the turnpike system collapsed, owing mainly to railway competition, the main roads reverted to parish responsibility. In 1862 parishes were grouped into Highway Districts, the records of whose Boards may be available. Roads next came under the control of the County Councils instituted by the Local Government Act of 1888. Improvements were made by the Road Board formed in 1909, and in 1919 this was succeeded by the Ministry of Transport, which took over responsibility for trunk roads and has more recently been responsible for the construction of motorways. It follows that records for twentieth-century development are to be found with the County Councils and with the Ministry of Transport.

Transport and urban expansion

An historical approach to the development of the geography of street patterns and traffic flows should include a study of changes in the methods of transport. This not only affects the type of road required (although many streets were not designed for the type of traffic they now carry) but also the distribution of population. Thus the tram and the workman's ticket on the railway enabled working-class housing to develop further from the place of work; the electric railway enabled suburbs to grow; and the motor car made long-distance commuting possible from places not served by rail and accelerated the emptying of residence from town centres. The development of country bus services increased the importance of towns as 'central places' and increased the centralisation of such services as education. Thus a study of the history of local transport undertakings is relevant to a study of the growth of a town and helps to explain many of its present-day features.

10. Distribution of population and urban growth

DISTRIBUTION OF POPULATION

Short-term changes

The flow of commuter traffic in and out of towns indicates that there must be considerable variation in the distribution of population according to the time of day. Other features also indicate such change—the number of shoppers on different days, the emptiness of some towns in holiday periods and the fullness of others, the thronging of people to football matches, the emptiness of streets in the early morning, the variation in the number of parked cars, and the mass exodus from factories when the hooter blows—to name but a few. These changes are very important in considering how they may be accommodated and what they mean in terms of the lives of the people concerned, but they are not easy to measure. Some ways have been outlined in the previous chapter, under 'Traffic Studies'. Much will have to depend on general observation, but some basic statistics are available and two sources are dealt with below.

Census of Population

When it comes to the question of density of population in terms of households—what we might call the 'sleeping population'—we have information in the Census of Population published in County volumes by H.M.S.O. The full census is taken only every ten years (starting in 1801). Another difficulty is that the figures for boroughs are given by wards, and these are too large, and therefore contain too much internal variation, for a map based on them to show a really close resemblance to the actual state of affairs.

The figures are normally mapped as dots, to an appropriate scale, and their distribution can be made closer to reality by leaving blank those buildings and open places obviously not used for housing, and by making some variation in dot distribution according to the types of housing in the area. This is not a strictly mathematical method and the maps so produced can be no more than a rough guide. More accurate maps could be produced if the statistical areas were smaller. We could, for instance, use the collecting areas, the enumerators' districts, instead of wards, and this information is available from the Registrar General for a fee 'if he so thinks fit'.

Electoral Rolls

A group of people whose exact home location can be found is formed by the 'over 18's', the voters on the Electoral Roll. This can be obtained from the Local Registration Officer, who is usually the Town Clerk. It is then easy to produce an accurate map of the distribution of electors, especially if the 1 : 1 250 map with house numbers is used as a base.

Such a map can be adjusted to show the total number of people in the house if we know the ratio between the number of electors and the total population in the ward, the *T/E factor*. The calculation and application of this factor is dealt with in detail by Hunt and Moisley in *Geography*, No. 207, vol. XLV, January and April, 1960, where two methods, one rapid and one more refined, are described.

The simplest method of calculating the T/E factor, or index, is to divide the total poulation for the ward as given in the nearest census by the electoral population given in the electoral lists. The T/E is then applied to the number of electors in each street, or each street block. In Glasgow in 1951 there were, Hunt and Moisley say, 1 089 767 inhabitants and 725 538 electors. The ratio was therefore 1.502 to 1, but in the wards the ratio varied between 1.864 to 1 and 1.246 to 1.

This T/E has considerable inaccuracies but it can be made more useful by separating households and institutions as follows:

1) Subtract from both the total population and the electoral population for each ward those who are not in private households. (In Glasgow the information was obtained from the Medical Officer of Health.) The T/E will then apply only to households.
2) In mapping, apply the T/E only to private houses. For institutions, enter the known total figures.
3) Produce a map by putting dots on dwellings and institutions on either the 1 : 2 500 or 1 : 1 250 map. In the Glasgow example one dot on the 1 : 2 500 map represented 5 persons. Before plotting, the map must be brought up to date by a field check.

Other population classes

These include ethnic, occupation, income, and religious groups. The figures are difficult to get, but some help may perhaps be had from Employment Exchanges, Churches, and Housing Authorities. Accurate surveys require personal interviews based on a sampling system,* but personally I do not feel that private surveys are to be encouraged as they are very liable to be resented.

* See Yates, F., *Sampling Methods for Censuses and Surveys*, Griffin, 1960.

URBAN GROWTH: PHYSICAL

Identifying the ancient core

For every town there must have been a starting point, and this ancient core remains embedded, not necessarily centrally, in the later growth. The present focus of the town is not invariably the original one, which may not always be easy to discover. In seeking the ancient core we should consider the following factors.

The street pattern

The ancient core may well have a more haphazard arrangement of streets than the newer areas. The early medieval city was largely a place of houses and gardens which became twisted and complicated. In some cases, however, such as Flint, Hull, and Stratford-on-Avon, the early town was planned to form a grid.

Street names

An important aspect of early towns was the market, and 'Market' or 'Cheap' streets are likely to indicate its location. In some cases, however, as in Bristol's Old Market, a market grew up outside the city walls to avoid the control of the guilds. Names such as 'Northgate' and 'Borough Walls' often indicate streets within the old defences, although we should remember that in the North and in parts of the Midlands 'gate' means a street (Old Norse *gate,* not Old English *geat*), and in some circumstances (Gateshead, for instance) it can mean goat.

Churches and castles

There is usually a cluster of churches in the ancient core, although some of these may have disappeared and can only be detected in street names or old maps and charters. Abbeys, however, were frequently on open land outside the city, although in Bath, for example, the Benedictine Abbey was inside the walls.

Castles were often built to overawe the town and to be a place of refuge, and were located outside the city walls. In other cases, such as at Ludlow, the walls and castle formed one defensive system. Elsewhere, the castle was within the town, as at Launceston. In some instances, such as Newcastle-on-Tyne, the castle came first and a new town was added to it.

Charters

These were normally granted after a town had gained some importance, and they usually contain descriptions of the bounds. It should be remembered that the granting of a charter could be the occasion for enlarging a town.

Access

Even in a town sited for defence it was necessary to get provisions in, and in the case of trading settlements access was vital. Thus a study of bridges and roads may give clues to the situation of the original starting point of town growth. The area around a bridge was often too marshy for settlement in early days and so the old centre may be on slightly higher ground some distance away.

Old maps

Although the oldest map is likely to be of the early seventeenth century, sufficient of the early pattern will probably have survived to give a good idea of the situation of the original settlement.

Archaeological discoveries

Although street patterns and plot-shapes tend to persist, old building foundations and other detail are now probably buried beneath the later town and can only be determined by excavation. If there is a local archaeological society you should approach them first with your queries; other information may be obtainable at a town or county museum, at a local university, or in the appropriate volume of the *Victoria County History*.

Age of buildings

In some cases, such as the Shambles (meat market) in York, old buildings are to be found in the ancient core, but frequently these have been replaced in the process of urban renewal and some of the newest buildings in the town may be in its oldest part.

Topography

The exact site of the settlement will depend upon the nature of the ground and the availability of water from streams, springs or wells. A careful study of geology and relief will help us to decide what was the most likely spot for the first settlement.

Expansion from the core

Having established the site of the original settlement and investigated the reasons why it was chosen, you should go on to map the way in which the town has grown. This is a useful exercise since it is an important guide to understanding the forces which have shaped the town and developed its internal pattern, or *morphology*. Morphology (from the Greek *morphe*, shape) is a term borrowed from biology where it refers to the study of the internal structure, or form, of animals and plants. It is not simply descriptive but is also concerned with inter-relationships. We will consider this in more detail in the next chapter.

A study of the growth of your town may have been published already, in which case your task is to check it in detail on the ground and to add any developments that have taken place since the original work was done. If no such study has been published, you will be doing pioneer work. The amount you can do will depend upon the quantity of source material available, but in any case a good deal can be learnt by observation in the field. The sources you can use have been summarised in Chapter 3 and here we will deal only with two methods—the use of maps and the use of field studies.

Mapping the growth

Find all the maps you can. Even if there is nothing before the nineteenth century you will be able to do useful work on Ordnance Survey maps alone, as these will give you a picture of nineteenth- and twentieth-century growth, probably the period of greatest expansion of your town. Note that the date to be used is not that of publication of the map but the date of its revision, which is printed at the foot of Ordnance Survey maps.

The maps, especially the earlier ones, or those privately printed, may be on a variety of scales. Trace a line in each case round the edge of the built-up area and reproduce these lines on a single map, preferably on the 1 : 10 000 scale. If possible, use shading or colouring to show which parts within these boundaries are mainly (*a*) industrial, (*b*) residential, (*c*) service (banks, shops, offices, etc.). If the functions of areas have changed during the growth of the town, you should prepare several maps, unless you can show the change in some other way, such as by cross-hatching in different colours. Changes in the administrative boundary of the town should also be shown. Outline adjacent built-up areas; they may later become incorporated in the town by boundary-extensions. Mark open spaces in green; they may become building sites.

Field studies in urban growth

Even if you have a complete series of original maps there will be a gap of some years between each, and new buildings may have been put up at any date between the revision of each map. A more exact date should be sought by studying the buildings themselves. Where maps are few and far between this fieldwork is even more important. The aim of such a study should be to produce a map of building dates or, where this cannot be determined, of building styles. A map showing dates of buildings is not a completely accurate guide to the history of the expansion of a town because, as we have seen in discussing the core, later buildings may be substituted for much earlier ones. Such urban replacement or renewal has

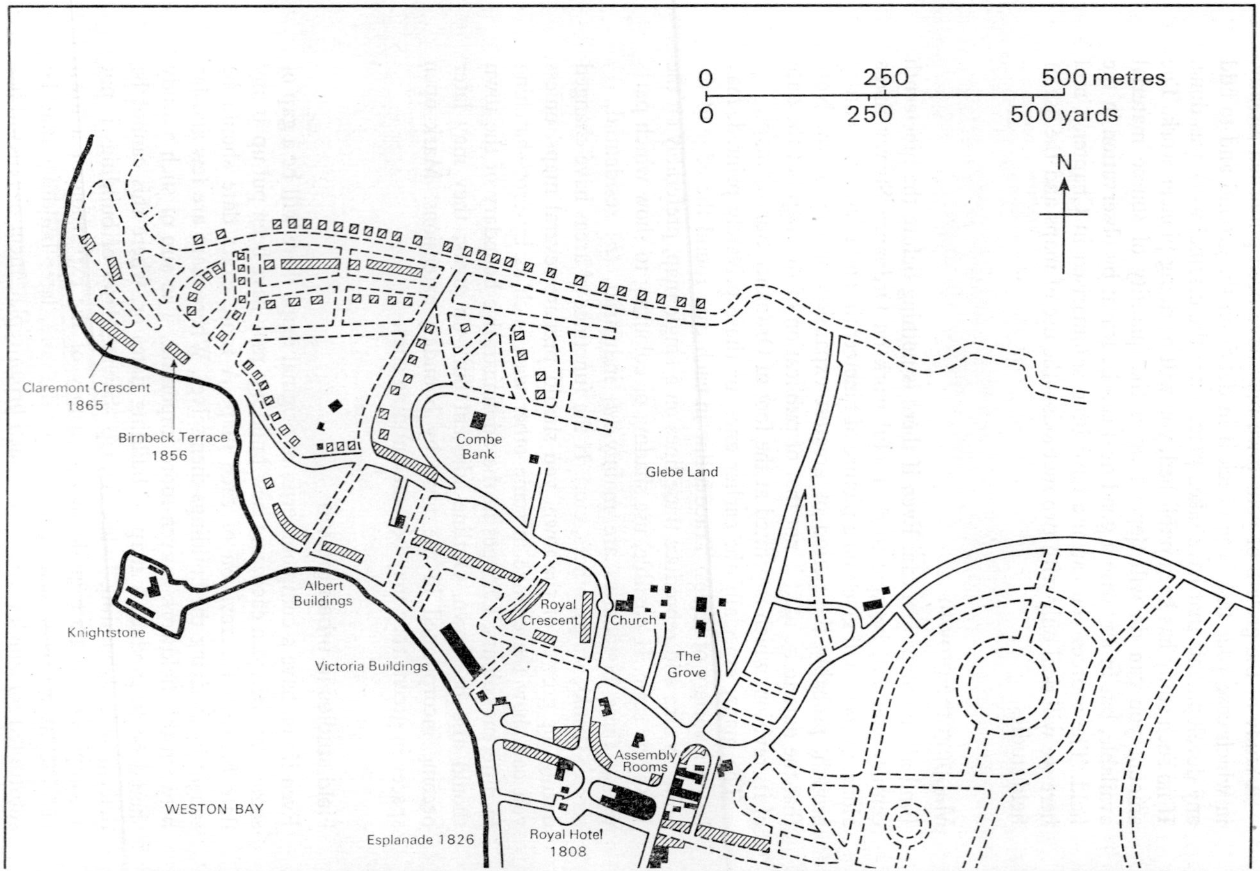
0 250 500 metres
0 250 500 yards
N
Claremont Crescent 1865
Birnbeck Terrace 1856
Combe Bank
Glebe Land
Albert Buildings
Knightstone
Royal Crescent
Church
The Grove
Victoria Buildings
Assembly Rooms
WESTON BAY
Esplanade 1826
Royal Hotel 1808

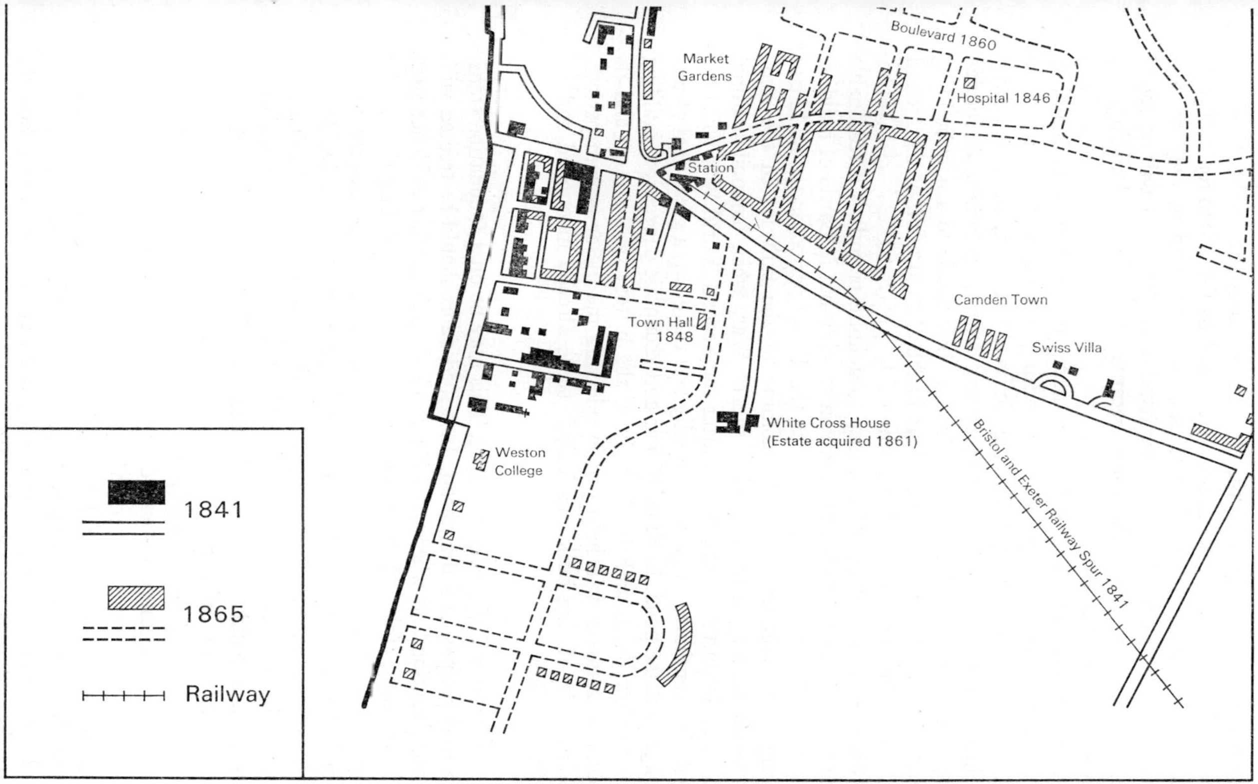

Figure 20 A growth map: Weston-super-Mare, 1841-1865
Based on the Ordnance Survey maps of the terminal years

taken place, for example, with the clearing of slums and in the rebuilding of bomb-damaged areas. Normally we can distinguish urban renewal from urban expansion for in the former case the new buildings will be surrounded by older ones. On the other hand a similar effect will be found when open areas within the town became available for building, by, perhaps, the sale of an estate.

In making our record it will not be necessary to date every building. There will be large areas, such as housing estates, which were quite obviously built at one time, and whole blocks of streets where the buildings are identical and obviously contemporary with each other. A sudden change in the pattern made by streets may be a guide to a new building period, but this may be due to changes in the configuration of the ground and should therefore be checked in the field.

Allocating whole blocks of territory to definite periods is a reasonable thing to do, since towns have not grown steadily but in bursts of building activity. Such bursts tended to occur in the Tudor period, in the middle of the eighteenth century, after the coming of the railways in the mid-nineteenth century, after the First World War, when 'council housing' became an important element, and after the Second World War when the population continued to increase rapidly and there was a great deal of war damage to make good. In times of war and economic depression, building tends to slow down or halt. A study of the history of the town and its population statistics will help you in selecting the major growth periods.

Sources for dating buildings include some already mentioned and are briefly as follows:

1) *A date inscribed on the building.* This may be on a foundation stone, a wall plaque, or a drainhead. Inscribed dates should be treated with some caution and where possible checked against other evidence such as building style. They may refer to a previous building on the site (may even have come from it), or to an event in the history of the building. Foundation dates of firms do not necessarily coincide with that of the building they occupy. Inscribed dates are useful in training yourself to develop an eye for building periods; it is very satisfying to date a building by its style and then find an inscription which confirms your opinion.
2) *The name of a building or street,* if it refers to an historical event or person (sometimes a local dignitary); for example, Jubilee Road, Coronation Street, Albert Street, Chatham Row, Waterloo Road, Caroline Buildings, Trafalgar Square. The street cannot be older than the thing it commemorates *unless the street was re-named.*
3) *A series of maps and/or directories* of different dates which show the first recording of a street or building.

4) *Title deeds* to buildings. Where the Corporation owns the property its legal department may be able to help.
5) *Newspapers.* To save much search you should have some idea of the approximate date of the building.
6) *Local histories.* These are most common in the nineteenth century and are most accurate for events that occurred in the author's lifetime. Statements about earlier events should be treated with caution unless backed with evidence.
7) *Estate records* where areas of the town were part of a private estate.
8) *Council minutes,* with particular reference to town developments.
9) *Planning authorities,* for post-war changes.
10) *Acts of Parliament* relating to town development.
11) *Architectural style* of the building. This is often all you will have to guide you, particularly if you are making a quick survey. Much help can be got from your experience of observing buildings and relating them to dates from the sources noted above.

REFERENCES

Gallion, A. B. and S. Eisner, *The Urban Pattern,* 2nd edn., Van Nostrand, 1963.

The first part deals with the history of cities, the second with planning. As an American book it tends to be weighted towards the American condition, but the authors also illustrate considerably from Britain and Europe. There is a wealth of pictorial illustration well worth studying for its own sake.

Haddon, J., *Discovering Towns,* Shire Publications, 1970.

Deals with town history, particularly with reference to the growth and appearance of towns.

Mumford, L., *The City in History,* Penguin, 1966.

This book was first published in the U.S.A. in 1961. Mumford is a prolific author with an engaging style who has been very influential in the planning world. The photographs and accompanying text deserve close study.

Savage, W., *The Making of our Towns,* Eyre & Spottiswoode, 1952.

A good, straightforward introduction to the historical development of British towns.

Summerson, J., *Georgian London,* Penguin, 1962.

Already referred to on page 81.

URBAN GROWTH: FUNCTIONAL

So far we have been talking in terms of the sheer physical growth of the town, with only a brief reference to the functions of the new buildings. Growth, however, is a response to a functional need, as contraction is the response to diminished need. If we are to explain the pattern of growth we must investigate demand, and we must also find out what land was suitable and available to meet it. New building may be in response to:

(*a*) Enlargement of an existing demand such as the expansion of an established industry.

(*b*) The development of a new demand, such as the starting of a new industry or the discovery of a new resource. For example, the phenomenal growth of Middlesbrough in the second half of the nineteenth century was largely due to the exploitation of the iron ore of the Cleveland Hills. Other examples are the coming of railway works to Swindon, motor-car works to Cowley, and chemical works to Billingham. In some cases, such as Port Sunlight, a whole new town was constructed for the new factories. In others, such as the New Towns, demand which would have arisen in old-established centres was directed to new ones.

In considering new or increased demands we should bear the following facts in mind:

1) Demands are often linked. New factories may bring about an influx of workers who will need the services of people such as shop-keepers, school-teachers, bus-drivers and builders.
2) Demands may originate outside the town. Increased paid leisure and improvements in communication, together with a change in leisure habits, create a demand for the services of tourist resorts and may turn little fishing villages into thriving towns. Improvements in communications may render a town much more accessible so that it becomes an important shopping centre for a wide area, or conversely it may be a 'dormitory' town from which people go to work in a bigger centre some distance away. So that work in the larger place creates a demand for houses in the smaller.
3) The balance and location of demand may alter considerably as time passes. In industrialised societies there has been a marked tendency in this century for the proportion of workers in service industries to increase at a considerable rate. Middlesbrough, quoted above, owes its existence to industry, but today over 50% of its employed people are in service industries; in 1964 the average for England and Wales was 55·4%. This change has caused many central residential areas to become converted to offices and shops. One of the common features

of town growth is the movement of residence away from the centre, and this movement has tended to create subsidiary shopping centres.

As we have seen, there is a tendency, known as *industrial* or *geographical inertia*, for activities to continue in the same area even when the original advantages of the site no longer apply. Thus Middlesbrough, quoted above, has continued as a steel town although local supplies of ore have been exhausted. Offices of different firms had to be close to each other when the most rapid communication was by messenger and they still continue to crowd the Central Business District of towns although they now communicate by telephone. Much of this concentration is due to the prestige of a 'good address' and also because certain places are connected in the public's mind with specific activities.

For the study of functional growth it is useful to compare the distribution of different types of land usage at different times and to trace the fortunes of single industries, or even of single streets. For example, Milsom Street in Bath, now a fairly expensive shopping centre, with several banks and restaurants, was originally a residential and boarding-house street. In 1791 there were 29 lodging-house keepers there, some with more than one establishment; in 1850 there were none, although the total for the town had increased. This indicates a considerable change in the social and functional structure of the city. Southgate Street, also in Bath, had eight public houses in 1791, six in 1850, three in 1900, and one in 1967.

The nineteenth century, with its rapidly increasing human mobility, was a time of considerable change in the internal pattern of towns. It is fortunate that this was a period when town directories were common, for these are our best and often our only source of information. By using them it is possible to trace changes in use throughout the years, and from this information land-use maps of past times can be constructed.

There are, of course, problems. Early directories may be selective, they may not give street numbers, they may classify by occupation only and not by streets. A street may have at some time been re-numbered so that No. 21 of 1870 may not be the No. 21 of 1830. A street may have been re-named—in Bath, the Horse Street of 1790 is the Southgate Street of 1800. A business may persist but expand some part at the expense of another; thus an 'Auctioneer, upholsterer, and agent' may in a few years be listed as an 'Auctioneer' or perhaps a 'Furniture dealer'. Also, names of occupations may change, so that a 'broker' becomes a 'pawnbroker', a 'cordwainer' a 'shoemaker', and a 'victualler' a 'publican'.

When further information is needed it may be helpful to consult contemporary newspapers for accounts of building operations, opening of new stores and factories, and advertisements giving more detail about the size and nature of some businesses. Old bill headings may contain a wealth of detail. The accounts of Walcot Poor House are preserved in the Bath library and include a Voucher Book into which are fastened all the bills which were paid. We find, for example, 'J. Little. Linen and woollen draper, Hosier, Haberdasher, Hatter & Tailor, Cleaveland Place —opposite Mr. Smith's Brewery—Walcot. Funerals completely furnished' and 'Fry, old established Brush, Mop, Patten, Clog & Rope-Mat Manufactory—Combs, Bellows, Tubs, Buckets, Twine, Line, etc., etc., 6 London Street, near Walcot Church.'

Sometimes in directories there are two entries for the same person, one for his residence and one for his place of work, and we must be careful not to confuse these. A complete account of the residences, though not place of work (unless the two coincide), is given in the original census schedules for 1841 and 1851, of which the latter is more detailed. These are kept at the Public Record Office, Chancery Lane, London W.C.2 and may be consulted there. It is also possible to obtain microfilm copies which can be read by putting them through a filmstrip projector, but such copies may cost several pounds and take several weeks to produce. There is no objection, however, to writing for information about the cost. The information is arranged by parishes and the names of the parishes required should therefore be quoted in your letter. Alternatively, Xerox copies can be ordered from specialist agents such as Phillimore & Co. Ltd., Shopwyke Hall, Chichester, Sussex.

Individual firms may be able to give you some information about their origins and history. They should be approached with courtesy and caution, remembering that you are asking them to do something extra outside their normal work. You should have studied as much as possible from outside sources before you approach them and should try to make your request as specific as possible. If you have found a bit of information about their early days and can quote this, it not only shows that you are a genuine worker but it may arouse the interest of whoever reads your letter. 'Have you got . . .?' is better than 'What have you got?'. Particularly useful are old letter-files, accounts, bills of lading, and plans of improvements. If the factory or business has been on the same site for a long time, a tour round it may show where the original buildings were and how the site has been developed.

11. Regions in towns and towns in regions

The final chapters of this book differ from the preceding ones, for instead of being concerned with the nature and distribution of individual elements within a town they deal with more general matters, namely:

(*a*) The formation of *regions* within towns by the co-existence and correlation of individual elements.
(*b*) The interaction of the town and the areas around it.
(*c*) The relationships of towns with each other.

Regions and classes

Geographers are still cudgelling each other over the question of whether regions actually exist. The attitude taken in this book is that they do, that they are visually apparent, and that one of the tasks of geographers is to describe and investigate them. Even if an opposing view is held, the regional concept is still a useful basis for town study, for an important part of scientific activity is the testing of hypotheses.

The hypothesis that a town interacts with the surrounding area is not, however, in dispute. Towns influence, and are influenced by, the region around them, which we can call the *hinterland* or *umland*; in some cases, such as ports, these influences may be very distant. This interaction is making it increasingly difficult to treat the town as a separate entity from the country, and this has an important bearing on the structure of local government when the *city region* has become a leading concept (*see below, page* 123). Town and village are now often closely related. In many cases villages owe their continued existence to the accessibility of a town; in others the town has engulfed the villages which may still retain traces of their physical and social structure.

An important factor in the development of an urban settlement is its relationship to other towns, and we shall see how this may affect their spacing and function. Such relationships also help us in classifying and ranking towns. Although each settlement is in some sense unique, there will be some characteristics which it shares with some other places, and the recognition of common features will enable a classification system to be devised. These classifications serve at least three purposes:

1) They help us to develop generalised concepts about the formation and distribution of towns.

2) They give us a measure of the degree of individuality of any particular town.
3) They serve as a guide to the forces which act on urban development.

What we are doing, in effect, is to change the scale of our studies. As we move from detailed individual scrutiny to wider concepts of whole regions, whole towns, whole sets of towns, we are working with maps—either on paper or in our minds—of smaller and smaller scale. The smaller the scale, the easier it is to generalise. Such generalisations are valuable but we must not lose sight of the large scale which depicts the immediate environment in which the individual lives. This question of scale is fundamental to geographical thinking and we must understand that the nature and appearance of geographical problems and geographical investigation alter with the scale on which we work. It is perhaps unfortunate that we use the terms large and small scale in two different ways. A large-scale map usually covers a smaller area than a small-scale one. A large-scale study usually covers a larger area than a small-scale one—or it can mean that the former is more detailed than the latter.

REGIONS IN TOWNS

Defining regions

If you have conducted surveys such as have been suggested you will find that in each case some sort of pattern emerges and strongly contrasted areas may be seen—poor housing and good housing, shopping and industry, dense parking and sparse parking, tall buildings and low, brick and concrete, dense building and scatter, and so on. In some cases a boundary may be sharply defined—a street or the middle of a street, a railway line, a river, a sharp break in slope, the edge of a housing estate. In others the elements may be inextricably mixed and it will not be easy to find a single descriptive name.

The difficulties of defining regions are not to be denied, but at the same time experience shows that regions do emerge and that if maps of different elements are superimposed a degree of coincidence emerges which indicates a set of *geographical* regions. This method is laborious but fairly simple; what will normally result is a number of regional *cores* surrounded by boundary *zones*. It would be possible, on the other hand, to feed all the information into a computer and ask the machine to give us all the various coincidences. Many of these could be rejected as combining too few factors, but where there is a coincidence between several characteristics this may be used as an indicator of a regional feature. Always, however, we must be beware of assuming that coincidence necessarily implies cause.

Recording by recognition

We will discuss later the reasons for seeking regions. For the moment I want to consider another approach to defining them, recording by recognition. After all, if a geographical region is something which can be seen, the sensible approach would appear to be to go into the field and look for it, rather than to sit in a drawing office and work it out as a kind of Identikit portrait.

Basically, the method is to work out a series of radials and travel along them by bicycle, car, or bus. Whenever the urban landscape changes, make a mark on the map and allocate a brief descriptive name to the new scene. The road will thus be divided into sections and further travel will be needed to check how the boundaries of change run between the radials. From this can be drawn a map of geographical (or townscape) regions. Then we must start to investigate why there are differences and why each region has a characteristic of its own.

For this quick method we can use the terms and abbreviations given on page 89 (flat front, even skyline, and so on), or we can enter brief descriptions or descriptive phrases. There is, as we have already seen, no standard terminology, but it may help to include here some of the main types of townscape (or perhaps *streetscape* would be better) you are likely to come across.

1) *Housing estates* of semi-detached two-storey houses, in gardens, with grass-verged roads in an often confusing pattern of loops and cul-de-sacs. The type of house tends to be standard over the estate, which may have been built by the Council or by private enterprise. Inter-war houses will tend to be rather square and flat-faced with metal-framed casement windows. Bay windows on the ground floor were also popular in this period. Immediate post-war housing may have a utilitarian look and contain some unusual materials. Later building tends to go in for picture windows and panels of wood, and also tends to give rather more provision for garages. In spite of the apparent uniformity of many estates (and, indeed, of much suburban building), which makes them easy to get lost in, a close study can reveal local differences which would necessarily be ignored in a general survey but which can make a study of the estate itself a useful exercise. As a blanket term for this kind of townscape we could simply use ESTATE or GARDEN ESTATE.

2) *Semi-detached or detached houses in gardens lining a main road*, with open country behind. The houses are similar in pattern to those in the estate but along some roads they may be rather larger and more varied. Ground-floor bays are common and there is frequent use of plaster and pebble-dash. This is typical of much inter-war building

and may be called RIBBON or BEADED. Victorian ribbon development tends to be in longer rows and may be called RIBBON TERRACE.

3) *Large detached houses in their own gardens* along main or minor roads. There tends to be a general impression of woodland. The houses often date from the horse-and-carriage age and are in a wide variety of styles from Suburban Balmoral to Stockbroker's Tudor.* This is really trying to have a country estate in a town and is appropriate to neither. We might call it SCATTERHOUSE COUNTRY. It is part of what Ian Nairn called 'Subtopia'.

4) *Terraces* of two- or three-storey houses with back gardens, facing narrow streets which form a grid pattern. These houses can vary a good deal according to the area, although they are consistent along the street. In some cases they will be quite substantial and may have bay windows, gables, and a deal of applied ornament. In others they may be Classical in style, with large porticos, and stucco finish—Lancaster's 'Kensington Italianate'. Many, however, will be rather mean, with flat faces and rarely more than a line of brick in a contrasting colour, or a bit of mass-produced carving stuck in over the door, to relieve the monotony. These types are all typical of Victorian development and cover large areas of our bigger towns. We can call them PLAIN TERRACE and FANCY TERRACE, or if the latter term is felt to be derogatory we may say PATTERNED TERRACE.

5) *Continuous buildings* which have a more or less unbroken line but are in a number of styles, largely caused by replacement of older buildings (so-called 'urban renewal') and infilling of gaps. These are difficult to generalise about and are often typical of central areas (the urban core). We might lump them together as VARIEGATED TERRACE.

6) *Unbroken ranges of buildings* outlining some geometrical shape such as squares or crescents. They are a particular achievement of eighteenth-century builders but have continued in various forms to the present day. The actual appearance of the enclosing terrace will depend on the building style and this may be added to the general title which we may call GEOMETRIC.

7) *Tall blocks of flats in landscaped open areas*. This is estate housing with the houses piled on top of each other and the gardens run together into a park. We might call it PARK FLATS, or PARK TOWERS where the flats are in fact in towers, or point blocks, as they are sometimes called.

8) *Tall blocks of flats by the sides of streets*. We may call these STREET FLATS.

* One of the expressive phrases coined by Osbert Lancaster in *Pillar to Post* (Murray, 1938).

9) *Streets of medium-sized shops,* usually with flats or offices above. These shops have usually been established in the altered ground-floors of houses, the alteration having taken place with little regard for the style of the building above or the shop fronts on either side, thus forming Main Street Jumble. Perhaps we can call it SHOP STREET, for it is the shop fronts that most catch the eye, but we really need to add some other descriptive term such as GENUINE GEORGIAN or NEO-GOTHIC.

10) *Streets of large stores,* often with offices, banks and places of entertainment. In a large town these tend to be *the* shopping centre and therefore the most congested and difficult to shop in. Such streets will often contain a good deal of rebuilding and refacing, and the buildings will tend to be larger than in 9) and to carry their function up through more storeys, perhaps on to the roof. There is liable to be a variety of styles. Even when wholesale destruction has allowed a whole area to be rebuilt at the same time, a master plan may not necessarily have been adopted. We may borrow the American term 'Central Business District', and call this streetscape a C.B.D. STREET. Or we might term it STORE STREET, or MAIN SHOP STREET.

11) *An estate, often municipally owned, of small factories,* usually near or on a main road. This is typical of many of the fringes of our towns. Some such estates, such as Slough, are very large; others are small. Sometimes they are called trading estates. They do not usually include housing, but housing estates have probably developed quite near. FACTORY ESTATE is a self-explanatory term.

12) *A region of large industrial buildings,* perhaps of only one firm. Such industry is often rather unpleasant in its output of waste, fumes and noise, and although Victorian housing may still surround it, the tendency has been for people to move further and further away from it. Later industry of this type, usually called 'heavy', has had its location controlled by zoning. We could use the term HEAVY INDUSTRY, although we might add HIGH or LOW to distinguish types of building, as between (say) a flour mill and a car factory.

13) *Tall blocks of offices.* These tend to be found mixed in with the other buildings of the C.B.D. and may not form a separate streetscape. If they do, we might use the term HIGH OFFICE or—to avoid a bad pun—simply OFFICE BLOCKS or OFFICE TOWERS.

The purpose of regional study

If we now ask ourselves why we should seek and set out these regions we may consider the following points:

1) Regions exist; a town is not a haphazard collection of varied buildings. Therefore if we are to give a true account of spatial relationships within our town, a geographical account, we must recognise and delimit these regions.
2) If we are to grasp the geography of our town, we must use some form of simplification. Structuring our material on a regional basis is such a simplification, and is meaningful and geographically sound.
3) The regions are the resultants of a variety of forces. If we are to understand how these forces work, as we need to if we are to control the future of our town in a satisfactory way, we must study their effects.
4) The spatial relationships between each region give us guidance about the way our town has grown. This is really a special case of the last point. It helps us to understand human motives and their results, so that we can learn from the past.

We cannot, of course, generalise from a single study, but we can test general theories against our own experience. For example, there are three main theories about the pattern of growth of cities. The first, and most often quoted, is the *Concentric Zone Theory*, developed in particular by E. W. Burgess in America. In its crudest form this says that cities grow by adding belts round their periphery and that these belts have characteristics of their own—so that from the centre outwards we are likely to find

(*a*) a Central Business District (C.B.D.),
(*b*) a 'twilight zone' of deterioration,
(*c*) poor residence,
(*d*) better residence,
(*e*) a commuter belt.

The second idea, also developed by an American, Homer Hoyt, is the *Sector Theory*. This was based on a study of rent values, and in the examples chosen it was shown that high rents, instead of being in a ring, were in wedges stretching out from the centre. This radial theory also ties in with the facts of development along main routes from the centre.

The third is the theory of *Multiple Nuclei* and is based on the fact that large towns, London for example, in growing swallow up existing settlements which may continue to retain some of their original characteristics. Often a town will extend its boundaries to include another settlement before it has actually been linked to it by building. In other cases nuclei may develop within the body of the city itself by the concentration of special types of activity, and in so doing may alter the characteristics of the area around it—a sort of contact metamorphosis.

A regional study of your town will show to what extent it accords with any of these three theories or may, indeed, reveal a structure which cannot be explained by any of them and requires analysis in different terms. One special case does not necessarily invalidate the general theory but in finding out why the theory does not apply you may arrive at an important modification. The study of Bradford-on-Avon in Appendix I shows a combination of Sector and Concentric development which can be explained in terms of topography.

Urban transects

These are included here because they are a useful way of illustrating regional changes within towns, but they also have a wider application and are helpful in exploratory surveys.

An urban transect is a survey of either all geographical detail or of selected features along a narrow band, at its narrowest a street width, chosen to pass through contrasting areas. With towns on rivers this can usually be done by going down one side of the valley, across the river, and up the other side—a Valley Section. Quite short transects can be useful if the line is carefully chosen. The transect will be made up of a series of straight sections, but should approximate to one master line.

The facts are collected as the observer walks along the line of the transect. If there are several observers they can either go as a group, with each person taking responsibility for observing a different feature—thus if Harry records land use, Fred may record architecture and Susan slope—or the transect may be divided into sections and each section allocated to a different person. A recording sheet similar to the one used for the land-use survey may be used, or a rough map may be made, the information being entered on the appropriate side of a centre column, as shown in the shopping survey. Usually the column is marked up the centre of the page, but in some cases it is more convenient to turn the notebook sideways, with the column running from left to right, and divide the page into columns, one for each type of observation, parallel to the centre line. The use of columns arranges the material conveniently and ensures that nothing is forgotten.

On the other hand, it can be helpful to make a descriptive record; for example:

'Along Disraeli Road starting at Beaconsfield Street. Red brick Victorian terrace (one dated 1870). Three storeys with bays and gables. Small front gardens. All private houses. Level slope. Wide street. No trees. Junction Gladstone Terrace.

Continues on left (east) as before. On right similar houses converted

Name of region	Hill St.	North St. crossroads	Upper Marsh Rd.	Lower Marsh St.
Land use	houses	small shops	houses	industry
Building type	terrace	terrace	terrace	small factories
No. of storeys	2 and basement	3	2	2 and 1
Architecture	early Vic. fancy	late Vic. plain	late Vic. plain	late Vic. utility
Wall material	stone	stone	brick	brick
Roof material	slate	slate or tile	slate	tile
Colour	grey	dark red	red	red
Gardens	small front	none	none	none
Street width	medium	wide	narrow	medium
Pavement width	medium	medium	narrow	narrow
Trees	none	none	none	none
Traffic density	medium	heavy	medium	light
Parking density	light	heavy	light	light
Slope	steep	level	gentle	flat
Geology	sandstone	sandstone	clay	clay
Cross-section	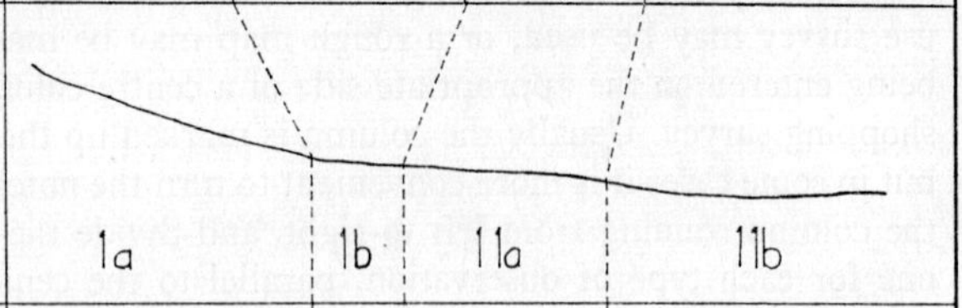			
Route map	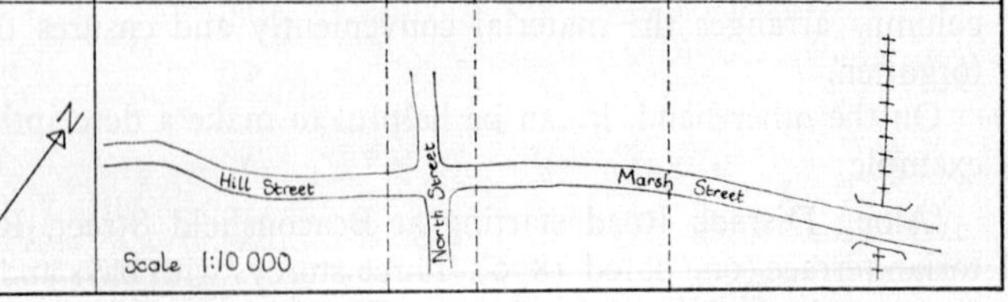			

into shops by building ground floor out over front gardens. Residence above. Mostly food and household goods. No large shops.'

This could then be written up in an extended form which could include comments on the reasons for the change shown, possibly the result of a central position in relation to the coming of electric trams. Incidentally, a verbal record such as this could be made on a portable tape recorder.

If the transect is to illustrate a single relationship, for example building development to physical features, presentation is simple. If, as is more usual, it is to show a whole range of features, then a more complicated form is used (*figure 21*).

TOWNS IN REGIONS

Field of influence

We have discussed regions inside towns, but the town itself is part of a larger region which may be delimited according to a number of different criteria. It may, for example, be administrative, a county perhaps; or economic, the area which supplies and is supplied by the town; or social, the area where people live who look to the town to supply education and entertainment and perhaps regularly read its newspaper. In fact you can abstract any one of the elements which go to make up the natural and cultural landscape and the social and economic life of the area and use it to delimit the region.

The *geographical* region will be one in which various elements go

---

Figure 21 (*opposite*) An urban transect

(*a*) Although an imaginary example this approximates to observations in part of Bristol

(*b*) The type of industry should be specified.

(*c*) Geology should be based on the Geological Survey map checked with local excavations.

(*d*) It would be more accurate to measure the widths of the street and pavement.

(*e*) Architecture could be further illustrated with photographs and sketches.

(*f*) It would be better to specify a time for traffic observation. For example, parking in IA increases considerably at night, and traffic in IIB becomes very dense for a short time when the factory workers come out.

(*g*) Parallel transects could be useful. In this case they could show that in one area of IIB factories have been cleared for high-rise flats, and in another, without Victorian factories, the clay lowland has been used for post-war light industries.

(*h*) This type of presentation is particularly suited to a large wall-display.

together to form a distinctive landscape. The *field of influence* of a town tends, however, to be larger than the purely geographical region, and increases with improvements in transport; it is better expressed by a more neutral word, such as the German *umland*. The practical problem is to find ways of measuring this sphere of influence. Some which have been used are as follows:

1) The catchment area of the town's schools. This will vary with the way in which the educational system is organised and is altered by changes in administration. For example, if the town has its own Local Education Authority it will not normally cater for children from the area outside its boundaries.
2) The distribution area of the town's daily or weekly newspaper.
3) The area covered by certain agencies, such as insurance, centred on the town.
4) The delivery field of certain shops.
5) The area within which town events are advertised.
6) The frequency of telephone calls to the town compared with those to other places.
7) The area for which the town provides certain services, such as hospitals.
8) The origin of goods sent to the town market, and the destination of goods sold there.
9) The frequency of buses to the town from outlying areas.
10) The distribution area for town wholesalers.
11) The journey to work from outside the borough boundary. Information can be obtained from the 'Usual Residence and Workplace' tables of the Census. Those for 1961 are based on a 10% sample.

When the boundaries of these various regions are drawn it is unlikely that they will coincide, but there will probably be sufficient agreement between a majority of them for a generalised outline of the town's sphere of influence to be drawn. Exceptions will call for special study and explanation.

Changes in the umland

It is also interesting to consider the alterations which have taken place in the umland due to the growth of the city. This is closely linked with the development of transport facilities; for example, the change of some places from primarily agricultural settlements to 'dormitories' for people who work in the town, the death of shops and services in the smaller communities, and the location of branch industries outside the town. Considerable changes have taken place within the last half-century and therefore information can be obtained from older members of the local community as well as from printed sources.

Comparisons can also be made between early census material and recent returns. Changes in land use are common, such as the increase of dairying and market-gardening (American 'truck farming') in the vicinity of the town.* Of particular interest is the history of the town's Common Lands and their enclosure.†

The umland can also be studied for factors that affected the city. These take a variety of forms. For instance there may be mining or agricultural products which have supplied industries with raw materials, surface features which have guided routes, and natural conditions which have inhibited the growth of rival settlements. Growth or decline may also have to be considered in a national, or even international context, as for example the decline of the West Country woollen towns, or of the port of Norwich. Decline may be relative, not absolute; in other words a town may continue to increase in size but at a much slower rate than comparable places. On the other hand the loss of one function, such as an industry, may be compensated for by the growth of another, such as a service, or a different industry. Thus in the little town of Calne, in Wiltshire, the total loss of a woollen industry was more than compensated for by the rise of a bacon-curing firm.

The term *city region* has come into use in referring to actual or hoped-for administrative units of local government, and the matter is dealt with in some detail by T. W. Freeman in *Geography and Regional Administration* (Hutchinson University Library, 1968). It has become of increasing importance since Local Authorities were given considerable planning powers because planning needs to be for larger and more geographically suitable areas than much of the present structure presents, and requires far more money than smaller authorities can afford. On the other hand, rural areas tend to be intensely suspicious of the motives of 'Big Brother' in the town, while town authorities frequently complain that they are providing services for people who are paying rates to a different authority. The whole question is too large to be discussed here‡ but it must be pointed out that local study of the facts is much needed, and useful work can be done in studies directed towards finding the relationship between towns and their surrounding areas and the extent of these relationships.

* For land use around a town, with particular reference to Von Thunen's theory, see Chisholm, M., *Rural Settlement and Land Use,* rev. edn. Hutchinson, 1968.

† See Hoskins, W. G., *The Making of the English Landscape,* Hodder & Stoughton, 1955; Hoskins, W. G. and L. D. Stamp, *The Common Lands of England and Wales,* Collins, 1963; and Haddon, J., *Local Geography,* Philip, 1964, page 31.

‡ See the Redcliffe-Maud Report on Local Government Reform, H.M.S.O., 1969.

12. The classification of towns

Size

This can refer to area or population, or a combination of both. Los Angeles occupies much more land than New York but has fewer people. In Somerset, Wells has approximately half the area of Yeovil but only one-third of its population; the average density of population in Wells is 12 persons per hectare (5 per acre), while in Yeovil it is 26 (10.7 per acre).

We can study the history of development of both population and administrative area. Our most accurate figures for both of these will start with the Census of 1801, quoted in the *Victoria County Histories* and elsewhere. Before that we have to rely on contemporary writers, tax returns, and such surviving charters as state the bounds. These charters unfortunately do not have maps but refer to landmarks which may have long since vanished. For Saxon charters we can refer to Birch, *Cartularium Saxonicum*, and Kemble, *Codex Diplomaticus*, and for municipal charters to the town records.

Early populations have to be deduced from tax returns and from Parish Registers. For the former see W. G. Hoskins, *Local History in England* (Longman, 1959), where he gives the statistics for forty-two provincial towns and discusses the sources for his figures. For the latter consult Hoskins again in 'The Population of an English Village, 1086–1801', *Transactions of the Leicestershire Archaeological Society*, vol. xxxiii, 1957, and the book *An Introduction to English Historical Demography*, edited by E. A. Wrigley (Weidenfeld and Nicolson, 1966).

In preparing a table of population growth, careful attention must be paid to boundary extensions for these will cause a jump in population which is not due to immigration or natural increase. Apart from this the table will normally show specific periods of rapid growth and will form a useful basis for the study of town development, indicating which periods require special attention. The table can also be expressed as a *rate of growth* graph, each increase being expressed as a percentage of the previous total. This is particularly significant if compared with national increases and with increases in adjacent areas. If it is worked out for wards, interesting differences in growth rates within the town may appear, but unfortunately ward areas tend to be too large for accurate location of areas of difference and the figures will have to be interpreted in the light of personal knowledge of the ward.

Various comparisons between the local town and others in the nation will help to establish the relative importance, or *rank*, in what Smailes has called the *urban hierarchy*. The simplest ranking is by population and it is indeed important to consider why our town is smaller than some and larger than others.

A good deal of investigation has gone into the question of whether there is some functional relationship between rank and size and a simple *rank-size rule* has been formulated. This states that the size of a town will be its rank number divided into the size of the first-ranking town; in other words, if the biggest town has 4 000 people, the fourth-ranking town will have 1 000. One pleasant thing about this is that if you have a list of towns and you graph the logs of the ranks against the logs of the populations, the curve, if the rank-size rule holds, will be a straight line (if you use log paper you can enter rank and population direct), and therefore the rule is not difficult to check. Results indicate that in some countries it holds fairly well (e.g. U.S.A.) and in others not so well (e.g. Thailand). In some cases it works over part of the list but not all (for example, it may work better if the largest city is ignored); in others it works better for large areas than for small (a country instead of a county). Mathematically there is the problem of determining how big the divergence has to be before it ceases to be significant. Even if the rank-size rule fails to work in a particular list, the ranking may indicate a definite grouping into size-bands (for example, villages, small towns, large towns, cities). Another useful exercise would be to run a rank-correlation exercise between ranking for population size and ranking of the same settlements for other features (*see pages 27–28*).

The difference in size will depend to a large extent on the jobs available in the town—not entirely, because some places attract retired people as residents, some have a high proportion of children, and others act as dormitories for commuters to larger settlements or to works located in adjacent rural areas.

Many of the jobs, increasingly so in a society with highly developed technology, are concerned with services rather than the production of goods. The number of jobs is therefore mainly affected by two aspects of the town—as a manufacturing region and as a service centre. The two are inter-related, as the town is not only a service centre for its umland but also for itself.

Services

In some towns the emphasis will be on industry, perhaps on one industry alone, and the fortunes of the town will fluctuate with those of the factories; but in others the emphasis will be on services and the town's prospects will tend to depend on its success in competing with other centres offering similar facilities. This depends to a large extent on accessibility and there will be a tendency for a grading of towns to appear —from the smallest, providing simple, basic requirements, to metropolitan cities offering a multitude of services, including those of the highest quality and those of the greatest speciality which it would not be profitable for a town with a small catchment area to offer.

With regard to shopping, people are prepared to make longer journeys for expensive articles bought at infrequent intervals and therefore the catchment area of supply for these is much larger than that for smaller regular purchases. Thus it pays the village shopkeeper to stock sweets but not grand pianos. The picture is affected to some extent by the amount of storage space the purchaser has; for instance, if he can store food in bulk, it may be more economical to make occasional visits to a supermarket some distance away than to pay regular visits to a local shop where the prices are higher. On the other hand there are non-financial factors such as social contacts and irrational preferences on which the small shopkeeper depends a good deal for his custom and which distort ideal patterns based on the logical decisions of 'economic' man.

The idea of towns as service centres, or *central places* (German *Zentralorte*), and their consequent distribution pattern has received much attention and has led to the development of interesting theories. Of these the best-known is that of W. Christaller in his book *The Central Places in South Germany*, originally published in 1935 and available in a translation by Baskin (Prentice Hall, 1966). A useful introduction to these ideas may be found in Chapter 3 of R. E. Dickinson's *The City Region in Western Europe* (Routledge, 1967).

Central place theory can also be applied *within* the town. A study of the location of different types of shops and services (such as banks) indicates centres of different *orders*, but the actual classification will depend on the criteria chosen. For example, how many banks are needed to move a centre from a lower to a higher order, what types of shops, how big the shops? How do you compare four shops and a bank with six shops?

Collins, in his contribution to *Frontiers in Geographical Teaching* (Methuen, 1965), suggests that as a basis for classification the numbers of establishments should be considered under the following headings:

1) All the shops which comprise the service area. (Collins himself, in a study of South London, made a broad classification into three grades: 300 or more shops, 200–300, and 100–200.)
2) Shops which specialise in five major categories—foodstuffs, household goods, luxury goods, and commercial services such as hairdressing.
3) Department, variety, chain, and multiple stores.
4) Establishments providing professional services, such as solicitors, accountants, estate agents, etc.

5) Banks.
6) Local and National Government offices.
7) Commercial offices.
8) Places of entertainment.

This information will have been obtained if the field survey method already suggested in this book has been followed, but we are still left with the problem of what combination of features goes to form a service centre of a particular order. In answer to this we would suggest that a fairly typical three-stage order might be:

1) Group of small shops selling mainly small household articles and food.
2) Similar group of shops, but including one or two stores and probably a supermarket.
3) Similar to 2), with the addition of some shops selling more expensive clothing, some selling large, relatively expensive articles such as furniture, and several providing personal services such as hairdressing or laundry.

It is probable that 1) and 2) will offer some banking facilities and that 3) will have a cinema and restaurant.

An American method is to divide the town into *neighbourhood centres* serving 10–20 000 people, *community centres* serving 20–100 000, and *regional centres* serving 100–250 000. 'The key facilitiy in a Neighbourhood Centre is usually a supermarket. About it may be grouped a drugstore, barber and beauty shop, baker, shoe repair shop, laundry and cleaning shop, and service station. The Community Centre will introduce a large variety store, or small department store, and augment the facilities of a Neighbourhood Centre with such establishments as an apparel store, hardware store, radio and repair shop, stationery store, restaurant and bar, bank, and branch post office. The distinction of the Regional Centre is the full complement of speciality shops and the wide selection of goods and services offered to the patrons, sometimes referred to as "Noah's Ark".'* This is a useful indication of the sort of division we can make, although there are considerable differences between American and British shopping habits.

The ranking of towns according to the facilities they provide as Central Places presents the same problems of classification criteria as does the ranking of service centres inside the town. Christaller obtained his ranking by determining the areas that towns of certain sizes *should* serve, on theoretical grounds, and then calculating the extent to which the town was able to fulfil these functions, expressing this in terms of an *index of*

* Gallion, A. B. and S. Eisner, *The Urban Pattern*, 2nd edn., Van Nostrand, 1963.

centrality. This index was based on the amount of telephone communication between the town and the area around and was based on the formula

$$Zz = Tz - Ez.\frac{Tg}{Eg}$$

where Zz is the index of centrality, Tz and Ez are the number of telephones and the number of inhabitants in the central place, and Tg and Eg are the numbers of telephones and people in the area theoretically served by the central place. This reliance on telephones has been strongly criticised, but the ranking which came out of it gave a reasonable approximation to reality in the area studied in Southern Germany and resulted in the following classification:

Grade of town	*Approx. pop.*	*Distance apart (miles)*	*Service area (sq. miles)*	*Pop. of service area*
I Market hamlet (*Marktort*) (M)	1 000	4.5	18	2 700
II Township centre (*Amtsort*) (A)	2 000	7.5	54	8 100
III County seat *Kreisstadt*) (K)	4 000	13.0	160	24 000
IV District city (*Bezirkstadt*) (B)	10 000	22.5	480	75 000
V Small state capital (*Gaustadt*) (G)	30 000	39.0	1 500	225 000
VI Provincial head city (*Provinzstadt*) (P)	100 000	67.5	4 500	625 000
VII Regional capital city (*Landstadt*) (L)	500 000	116.0	13 500	2 025 000

The areas served by each of these centres is considered as hexagonal, formed by the intersection of circles around each centre, with further centres at the corners of each hexagon. The shape will be distorted by such features as topography, but it would be an interesting exercise to compare the distribution of other towns in relation to your own, and according to their size, to see how far they accord with the theoretical pattern.

An English classification based on services is one by A. E. Smailes in 'The Urban Hierarchy in England and Wales', *Geography*, vol. xxix, 1944. He distinguishes the following types of centre:

Major cities (e.g. London, Bristol, Hull). These have a variety of services of national importance, such as a university, regional offices of Government departments, etc., and major regional services such as a large general hospital, a stock exchange, and a daily morning paper.

Cities (e.g. Southampton, Carlisle). These have a wide range of services but a smaller area of influence.

Minor cities (e.g. Bath, Aberystwyth, Dorchester). These have even smaller service areas and include places where service is less dominant; cities of the latter type are classified as industrial, county or resort.

Towns (e.g. Trowbridge, Dolgellau, Stroud). Although small, these have the five features taken as the criteria for a town—a secondary school, a cinema, a weekly paper, a hospital, and a group of three or four banks.

Sub towns. Lacking one or more of the five features.

Urban villages. Intermediate between the rural village and the town. In classifying your own town, consider other towns in the vicinity and attempt an explanation of their geographical relationship to each other. Such relationships will help you in considering whether your town is likely to move, in time, into another category.

Function

Although the service element is important, it is not necessarily the major feature of the town and it is therefore of interest to consider a classification by function. The simplest measure is the percentage of workers employed in each principal activity. This can be taken alone or compared with the national average. The figures can be obtained from the Registrar General or may be available at the council offices.

An influential method of classification along these lines was made in America by Chauncy D. Harris in 'A Functional Classification of Cities in the United States', *Geographical Review*, XXXIII, January 1943, reprinted in Mayer and Kohn, *Readings in Urban Geography* (University of Chicago Press, 1959). Harris used nine classes, as follows:

M—*Manufacturing*. M^1 subtype: employment in manufacturing equals at least 74% of total employment in manufacturing, retailing and wholesaling—and manufacturing and mechanical industries contain at least 45% of gainful workers. M^2 subtype: as for M^1 but figures 60% and 30–45% respectively.

R—*Retail Centres*. Employment in retailing at least 50% of total employment in manufacturing, wholesaling and retailing, and at least 2.2 times that in wholesaling alone.

D—*Diversified.* Employment in manufacturing, wholesaling and retailing is less than 60%, 20% and 50%, respectively, of the total employment in all these activities, and no other special criteria apply. Manufacturing and mechanical industries with few exceptions contain between 25% and 35% of the gainful workers.

W—*Wholesale centres.* Employment in wholesaling is at least 20% of the total employment in manufacturing, wholesaling and retailing, and at least 45% as much as in retailing alone.

T—*Transportation centres.* Transportation and communication contain at least 11% of the gainful workers, and workers in transportation and communication equal at least one-third the number in manufacturing and mechanical industries and at least two-thirds the number of the gainful workers (applies only to cities of over 25 000.)

S—*Mining towns.* Extraction of minerals accounts for more than 15% of the gainful workers (apples only to cities of over 25,000). For cities between 10 000 and 25 000, a comparison was made of mining employment figures made available by counties only with employment in cities within such counties.

E—*University towns.* Enrolment in schools of collegiate rank (universities, technical colleges, liberal-arts colleges and teachers' colleges) equalled at least 25% of the population of the city.

X—*Resort and retirement towns.* No satisfactory statistical criterion was found. Cities with a low percentage of the population employed were checked in the literature for this function.

The advantage of this classification is that it is tied firmly to statistics. The disadvantages, apart from the mathematical work involved, are that the statistics may be unobtainable or incomplete, that they may be available only under unsuitable or variable classification, and that the final result depends on Harris's choice of percentages, which is to some extent intuitive. Another disadvantage is that as a descriptive system this allows only *one* major activity to the town.

Another American system which is more generally descriptive was published by Howard Nelson in *Economic Geography,* vol. xxxi, July 1955, and is also reproduced in Mayer and Kohn. It is again based on the proportion of labour forces engaged in various activities expressed as a percentage of the total labour force in the town, but this is compared with the percentage in the other towns studied (Nelson took 897 American cities). Thus if a town has a much higher proportion in mining than the average it may be considered as a mining town. The question was then, how *much* of a mining town is it? The mathematical answer chosen was to express it in the number of standard deviations from the mean. Thus our mining town might be M2 if it worked out as between 2 and 3 standard deviations. The activities chosen as significant are the following: Mining (Mi), Manufacturing (Mf), Transportation and Communication (T), Whole trade (W), Retail trade (R), Finance, Insurance and Real Estate (F), Professional service (e.g. education, medicine) (Pf), Personal service (e.g. hotels, entertainment) (Ps), and Public administration (Pb).

Thus Laramie came out as T2Pf2Pb2, that is, as a town where transport, professional services, and public administration are all major activities.

Social factors

If in classifying towns we extend our attention to the many other variables which give it character, particularly human and social factors such as ethnic groups, standard of education, class structure, and state of health, we are presented with a formidable task in sorting and arranging our material.

One approach is by *factorial analysis*, where the variables are studied for inter-relationships and can thus be structured to reduce the large number of variables to a few significant groups. This is a process which needs the service of a computer. The method can be studied in *British Towns* by C. A. Moser and W. Scott (Oliver and Boyd, 1961). In this work for the Centre for Urban Studies, University College London, 57 variables were reduced to five main factors: Occupation; Social class (professional, intermediate, skilled, partly skilled, unskilled); Voting; Health; Education. The book is worth consulting for the insight it gives into the economic and social structure of towns, even if the mathematics may be daunting.

Site

This is an earlier but still important approach to classification. The disadvantage is that the groupings tend to be extremely broad and that in any case the town may have outgrown the control originally exercised by the physical circumstance of its position. Griffith Taylor, as an unashamed —though sophisticated—determinist, naturally placed considerable importance on physical site in his *Urban Geography* (Methuen, 1949). His detailed examples are well worth studying but his classification is very broad, consisting of only:

Hill towns—e.g. defended hills, cuesta towns, plateau towns, and towns in mountain corridors, passes, and gates.

River towns—at falls, in meanders, on terraces, deltas, fans, and islands, and away from the river but in the valley.

Seaports and lakeports—including towns on rias, fjords, and roadsteads.

Plains towns *Desert towns*

Many writers have discussed the importance of siting—W. G. East, for example, has an interesting chapter in his *The Geography behind History* (Nelson, 1965), where he quotes la Blache—'Man organizes the site prepared by Nature, so as to enable her to fulfil his needs and desires'—and a study of these suggests a broad classification similar to that made by Taylor. We may summarise it as follows:

River towns

1 At falls, e.g. Schaffhausen
2 At other breaks in navigation, e.g. Norwich
3 In meander cores, e.g. Durham
4 On one bank, using the river as defence, e.g. Exeter
5 On river terraces, e.g. Bath
6 At major river confluences, e.g. Koblenz
7 Where a tributary enters the main stream, e.g. Bristol
8 At fording and/or bridging points, e.g. London
9 On deltas, e.g. Venice
10 On river islands, e.g. Paris
11 Where rivers pass through gaps, e.g. Guildford
12 Estuaries where a deep water channel approaches the bank, e.g. Hull
13 In deep valleys, e.g. Stroud

Hill and mountain towns

1 Plateau-top, e.g. Birmingham
2 On groups of hills, e.g. Rome
3 In mountain basins, e.g. La Paz
4 Mountain gap towns (that is, on the mountain side of the gap), e.g. Banff

Coast and lakeside towns

1 On hill-girt bays, e.g. Dover
2 On flat coastlines, e.g. Harwich
3 On peninsulas, e.g. San Francisco

Plains towns

1 By a gap, e.g. Milan
2 At junction of plain and highland, e.g. Manchester
3 In an open plain, e.g. Ankara
4 Dry-point towns in a marshy area, e.g. Ely

Many towns will combine a number of these features and it may be impossible to say which was dominant. We must remember that in some cases economic or political factors cause a town to be built in a place that has few natural advantages. Washington D.C. was once 'that Indian place in a swamp'.

Townscape

Much less has been done about townscape description and classification. Mumford, following Geddes, classifies city development into Eotechnic (which Jones and others call Pre-industrial), Palaeotechnic (industrial) and Neotechnic, with their characteristic forms. Stimulating as these ideas are, they remain—like many memorable terms he coins or borrows (Anti-city, Baroque city, Megalopolis, Necropolis)—too broad and sweeping for our purpose here. A similar breadth attaches to Ewart Johns's division of townscapes into Medieval, Classical and Romantic.

An interesting idea was put forward by Smailes in 'Some reflections on the geographical description and analysis of townscapes', *Transactions of the Institute of British Geographers*, 1955. He classified urban landscapes in terms of *texture*, and distinguished *block clumping* (dense pattern of high buildings), *ribbing* (terrace housing), and *studding* (scattered units such as tall blocks of flats in landscaped open space). Perhaps we might add *shaping* for townscapes where geometrical forms are enclosed by buildings. This is a view from outside or above, rather than from within, the view of the outsider rather than the inhabitant, but when we consider the scale we must choose in order to look at a set of towns as a whole it becomes clear that any close-up is too restricted for our purpose.

This problem of scale applies to the townscape descriptions we have suggested earlier in the book. The whole essence of these was that they were the view of the man literally in the street, and we emphasised the diversity of townscape regions *within* a town. Even a very small town with consistent architectural style is likely to have an era of post-war housing on its fringe which from the point of view of townscape could hardly be included in the same classification as the rest of the town. Surely, our detailed study of townscape will emphasise the *uniqueness* of places and demonstrate the tremendous amount we lose when we submerge these vital qualities of individuality under a blanket classification, and what we lose when we cease to build 'in the spirit of the place'—which does not mean in slavish imitation of past styles. If we need a town classification by townscape, and I doubt it, I will venture into the field with the following remarks:

(i) It can apply only to the heart of the town.

(ii) It must concern itself with three salient features:
- (*a*) the colour/texture of the buildings—dark or light.
- (*b*) the pattern of the streets—close or open.
- (*c*) the style of building—Classical or Romantic.

On the whole the *open* pattern goes with *Classical* styles, the *close* with Romantic, but if we are going to include neo-Gothic with Gothic (for example), as we must if we are to keep our classification simple, then a Romantic style may be associated with an open pattern. This gives us eight classes:

1) Open, dark Romantic
2) Open, light Romantic
3) Close, dark Romantic
4) Close, light Romantic
5) Open, dark Classical
6) Open, light Classical
7) Close, dark Classical
8) Close, light Classical

This could be discussed at length but I will add only one thing. Strictly speaking, today's buildings are still in spirit either Classical or Romantic but the terms would not be applied in common speech. Instead, people would say 'Modern'. Unfortunately today's Modern is tomorrow's Traditional. If, therefore, we have to use an extra word to describe the 'modern' fashion, I would—as I have already said—prefer a term such as Rectilinear.

APPENDIXES

Bradford-on-Avon: the two main building types of the core.

Centre Gable house: stone mullions, dripstones, coursed rubble, stone tiles (sometimes replaced by slate or tile). *Right* Parapet house: Straight skyline, sash windows, ashlar, string courses. Note roof—an older building may have been re-fronted.

APPENDIX 1

Regional town study: an example

Bradford-on-Avon, in Wiltshire, is a small town, an Urban District not a Borough, of some 7 000 inhabitants. It has industry, shops, offices and a variety of housing dating from the seventeenth century to the present day. The quick method of recording was used and the fieldwork, on foot, took a day. I used a 1: 10 560 map clipped to one side of a board and a sheaf of foolscap clipped to the other, on which I drew enlargements of portions of the 1: 10 560 map as I needed them and then added the relevant notes. Half-way through I bought a small guide to the town as it contained a map in which the streets were named. I also took photographs and made sketches.

It soon became evident that the main building types were as follows:

1) *gabled* buildings, often with the roof axis end-on to the street, and with stone mullioned windows. These buildings were of a grey limestone, coursed, but in small blocks. They were usually intermingled with later styles, and were most common in the middle of the town. They were mainly of the seventeenth century.
2) *parapeted* buildings with sash windows and triangular pediments over doorways. Sometimes there was surface moulding in the form of pilasters. These buildings were mainly in rows but there were a number of larger separate houses in the same style, which is eighteenth-century. This type was found mainly in the centre but extended along some radials. Many were built in large blocks (ashlar) of the same grey limestone noted above.
3) *larger, more ornate buildings* of various styles; for example the 'Jacobethan' town hall, now a Catholic church, and the castellated fortress of the Ale and Porter Stores. These were all in limestone with one exception which was brick. They were later Victorian, and were all in the central area.
4) *Long, bay-windowed terraces* ribboning the roads, or larger blocks beading them. These were Victorian and had such names as 'Beaconsfield Terrace', 'Albert Terrace' and 'Gladstone Villas'.
5) *Estates* infilling between main roads. These were mainly of semi-detached small houses with gardens, and were either inter-war or post-war. Small patches of similar houses in-filled between some of the Victorian development. Most houses were of either limestone or reconstituted stone.
6) Large, grey stone factory buildings down by the river.

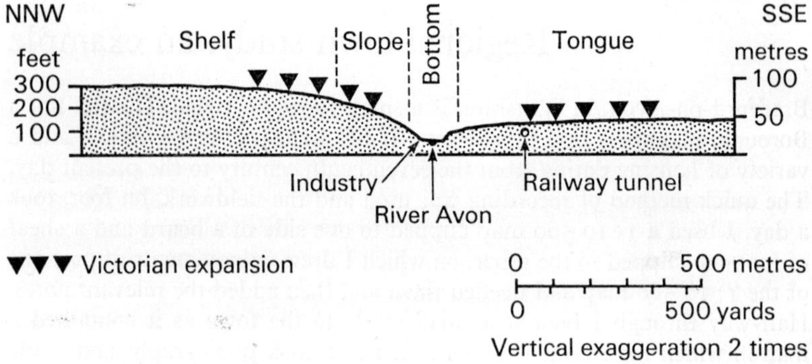

Figure 22 Cross-section of Bradford-on-Avon
Based on the O.S. 1:10 560 sheet ST 86 SW

Exceptions to the above categories did not seriously disrupt the general pattern. They included:

(*a*) A small Saxon stone church which had become embedded in later buildings and was not recovered until the late nineteenth century.
(*b*) A scatter of churches and chapels, mainly eighteenth-century Classical or nineteenth-century neo-Gothic.
(*c*) Two half-timbered, gabled houses with carved bargeboards, embedded in the Shambles in the centre of the town.
(*d*) An Elizabethan manor house, 'The Hall'—interesting but inaccessible.
(*e*) An eighteenth-century 'Gothick' mansion.
(*f*) A 'cottage orné', all tree-trunk pillars, pointed windows and thatch.
(*g*) A massive Victorian brewery, disused, away from the riverside industry, set in the side of the hill.
(*h*) An imposing eighteenth-century wall, built originally to bound a town estate.
(*i*) A gasworks, which now stores but does not make gas.
(*j*) A railway station and goods yard.
(*k*) A late Victorian neo-Baroque Grammar School down by the river, and a substantial neo-Gothic Board School up on the hill.

It was perfectly feasible to note these special details during the general survey and they can be the basis of future detailed work, but we are here concerned with the general pattern and this may be introduced by a brief consideration of the town topography as it became evident to my leg muscles.

The site is indicated in the name—it is by the Broad Ford through the River Avon and is situated where the river cuts through a tongue of land at the foot of the Jurassic plateau which can be taken as the extreme south of the Cotswold region. To the south of the river, the tongue rises to only 150ft (about 45m), but it falls very steeply to the river on the east where this small scarp has inhibited building; its slope to the ford (now the bridge) is gentler but evident. The slight rise would lift the houses above flood level and was also sufficient to cause the railway to disappear into a tunnel; the Kennet and Avon Canal, however, got across by using a lock and looping south to follow a tributary valley. Beyond the narrow, flat, flood plain of the river the land rises very steeply before flattening out again to a 'shelf' (*figure 22*).

The nucleus of the town is an hour-glass shape north and south of the bridge, with the greatest development, including the shopping centre and hotels, on the steeper ground to the north. Industrial development, originally based on water power, spread along the river, mainly east of the bridge (*figure 23*).

Eighteenth-century development consisted largely of urban renewal in the centre with some east-west extensions along the contours to the north of the river, and with some separate mansions, especially in the industrial region. Victorian expansion followed the coming of the railway and there is a marked change in housing style south of the line. The main development was along the Trowbridge road as it follows the tongue; radially northwards (rather more unevenly); and in a certain amount of renewal in the shopping centre. Post-1918 housing is to be found mainly on the tongue and on the 'shelf' to the north. The tongue has also been used for recreation grounds.

A distinctive area is that of Newtown, Middle Rank, and Tory, three close, parallel ranks on a hillside to the west of the core, so steep that the streets are connected by steps and houses with three storeys have only one at the back. The distinctive nature of the layout, its comparative isolation, and the name 'Newtown' suggest a particular development scheme at some date later than the core and possibly in relation to the eighteenth-century boom in the cloth industry. On examination, however, it is seen that the streets are a mixture of seventeenth- and eighteenth-century styles (both early and late), and documentary evidence shows the name to be at least as old as 1640, while St. Mary's chapel, Tory, contains a fifteenth-century window and is reputed to be on the site of a Saxon chapel of 652. Moreover, although very difficult for building, the area is closer to the Saxon Church, the Parish Church (part Norman) and the well at Tory which used to supply the town; and at the foot of the hill the contours come

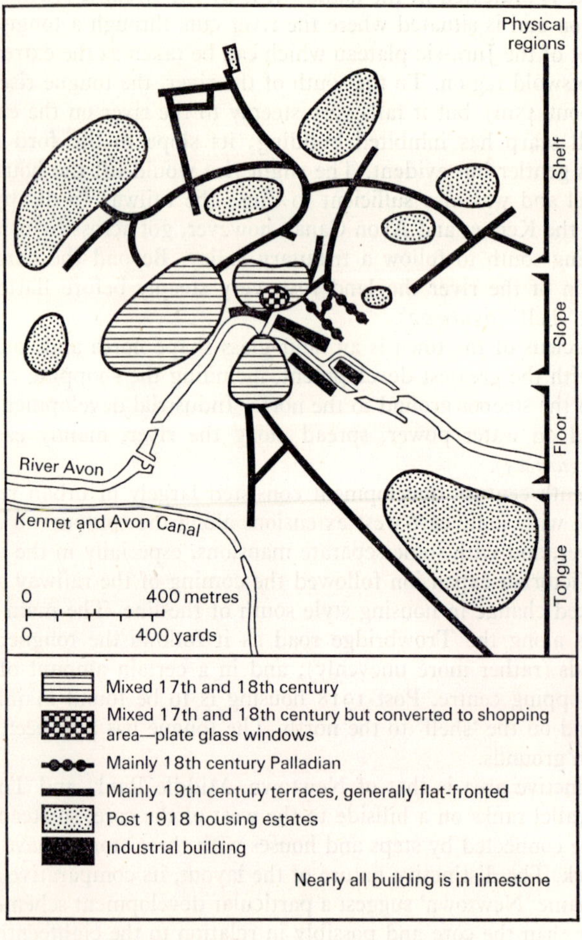

Figure 23 Bradford-on-Avon: townscape regions
Based on the O.S. 1:10 560 sheet ST 86 SW

closer to the river than they do at the bridge. It is also notable that 'Newtown' is in fact a common Saxon settlement name. Have we here the original core? Without further investigation and evidence this is a fruitless speculation, but it does show how ideas for future work can arise out of a brief survey.

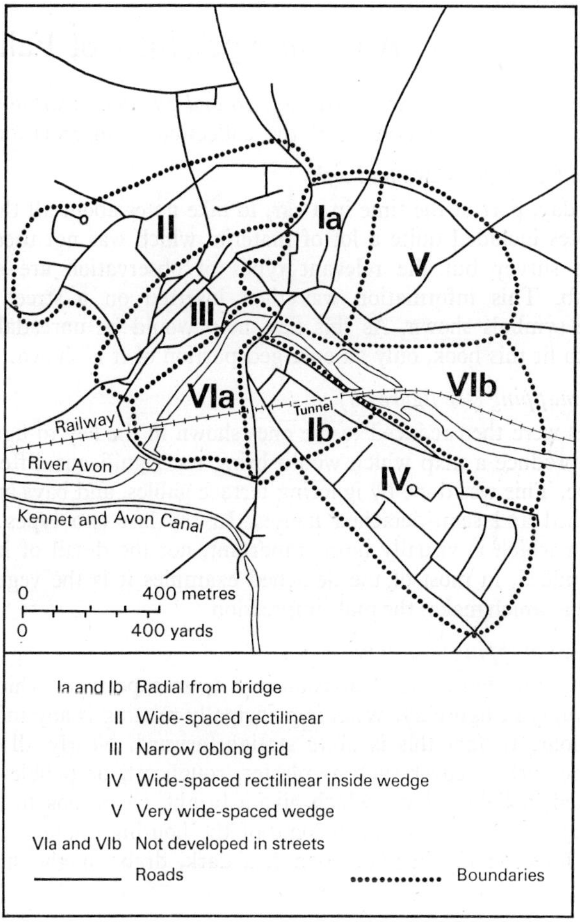

Figure 24 Bradford-on-Avon: street patterns
Based on the O.S. 1:10 560 sheet ST 86 SW

Finally, it is interesting to see the degree to which the street-pattern regions worked out from the map *before* the survey correlate with the townscape patterns which emerged from the survey (*figure 24*). Street-pattern maps are a very useful guide to planning the routes to be taken in fieldwork.

APPENDIX 2

A townscape study of Falmouth

The three maps that follow (*figures 25, 26 and 27*) demonstrate a method of progressive generalisation, after the collection of information.

Fieldwork (*see figures 25a and 25b*)

It took a day, part of the time in a car, to take notes about all the streets. These notes included quite a lot of material which was not used for the landscape survey but the relevant types of observation are shown in figure 25b. This information was then inserted on a street map by using the symbols shown. As this first map would be unreadable when reduced to fit this book, only an enlarged portion of it is shown.

Detailed mapping (*see figure 26*)

The types were then reduced to the ones shown in the key to figure 26 in order to produce a map which would bring out significant differences in townscape. This was done by ignoring terrace gables, and bays and gables on detached and semi-detached houses. In the last two types it is the separation which is visually most important, not the detail of individual houses; indeed, in most of the detached examples it is the vegetation in the gardens which makes the most impression.

Generalised mapping (*see figure 27*)

Figure 26 indicated a broad division into townscape types which is presented simply in figure 27. What is principally missing is any information about colour. In fact this is quite straightforward. Nearly all buildings have some surface cover such as plaster, roughcast, or pebble-dash and are painted in light colours which give a bright, clean look to the place. The exception is to be found in some of the housing estates where, presumably for economy in maintenance, a dark, drab, roughcast is used.

Analysis

The townscape regions fit in well with the historical development of the town, which mainly dates from the early nineteenth century. Terrace housing spread along the harbour front, fringed the hills to the north, and spread up the central valley. Later terraces of a more varied kind developed on the southern plateau. With the decline of the harbour in late Victorian times came a development along the land behind the beaches to the south. This consisted mainly of villas and hotels. The inter-war period saw the building of semi-detached houses and bungalows on the land to the west and around Beacon Hill to the north.

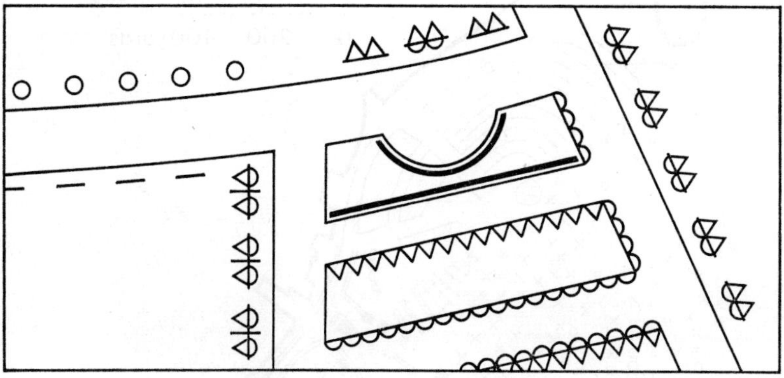

Figure 25a Falmouth: townscape 1
Enlarged portion of first map made from field notes

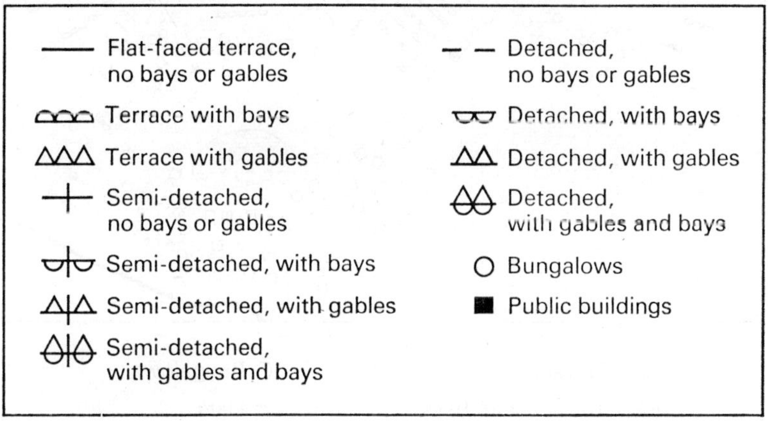

Figure 25b Symbols used for first townscape map

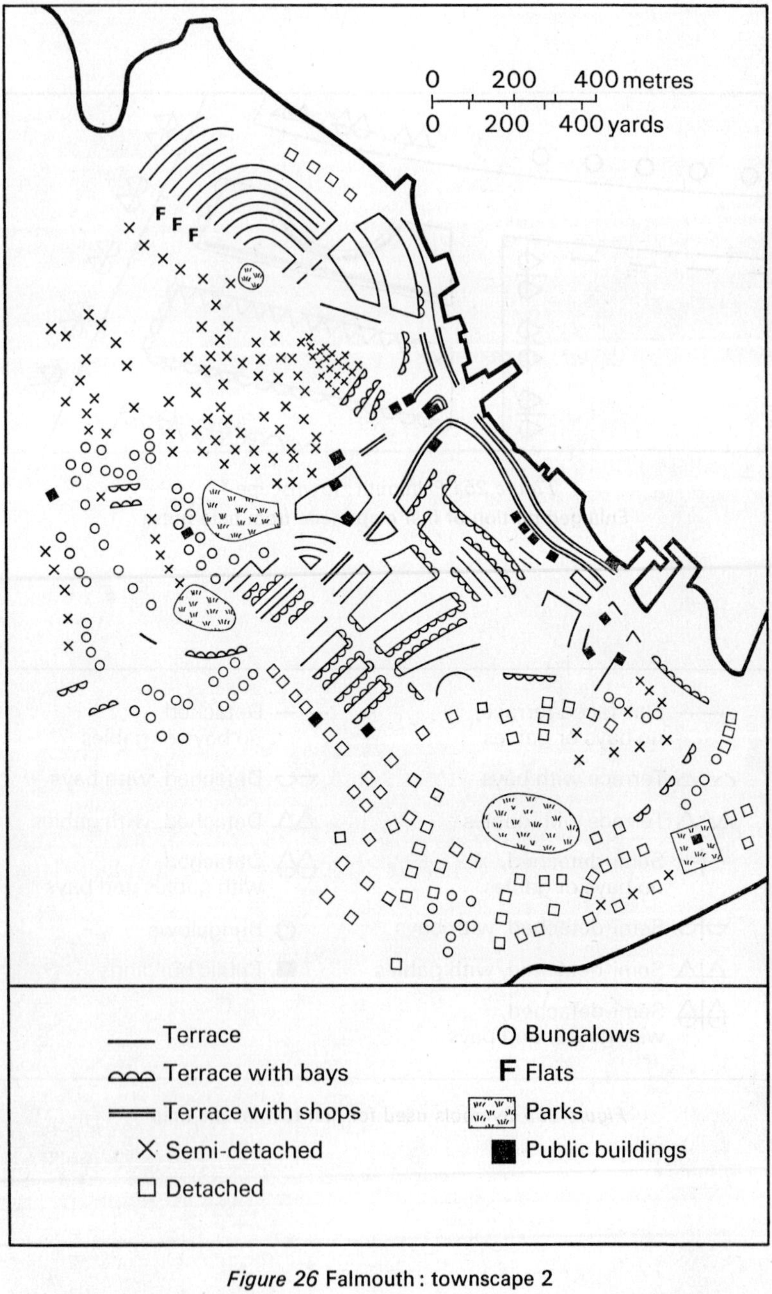

Figure 26 Falmouth : townscape 2

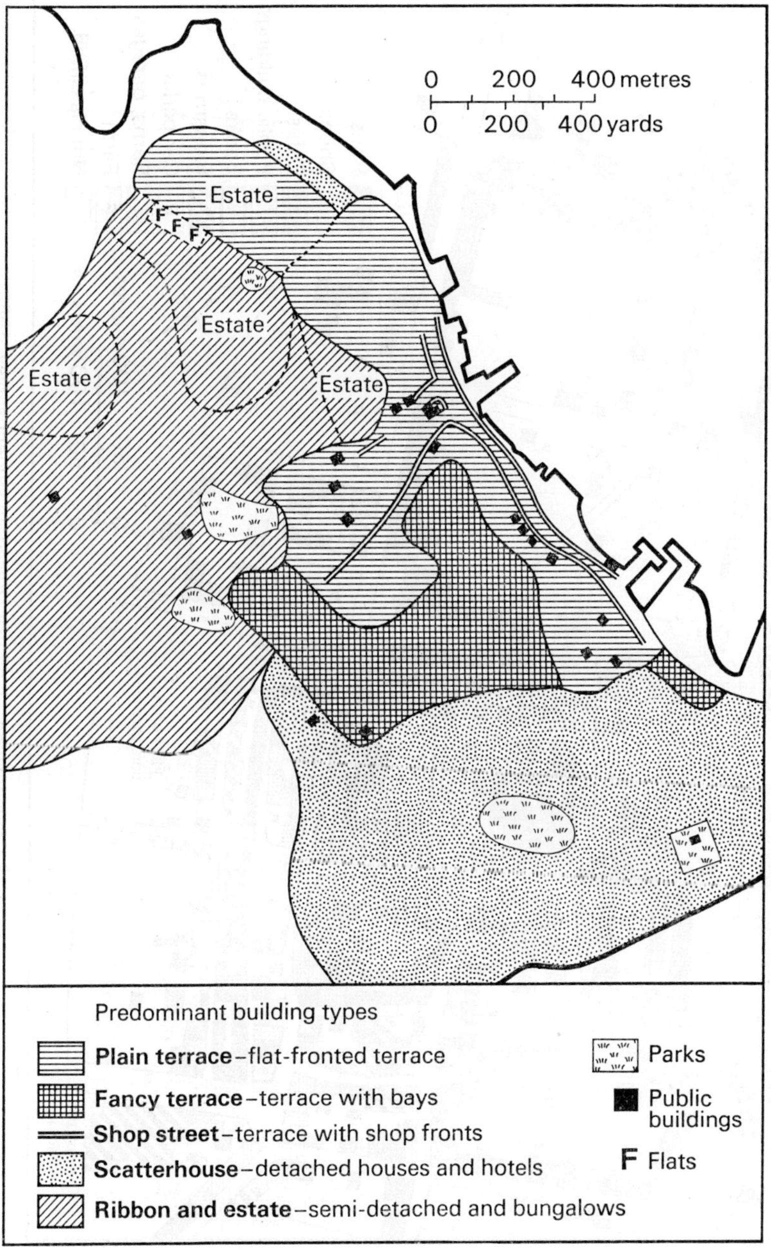

Figure 27 Falmouth: townscape 3

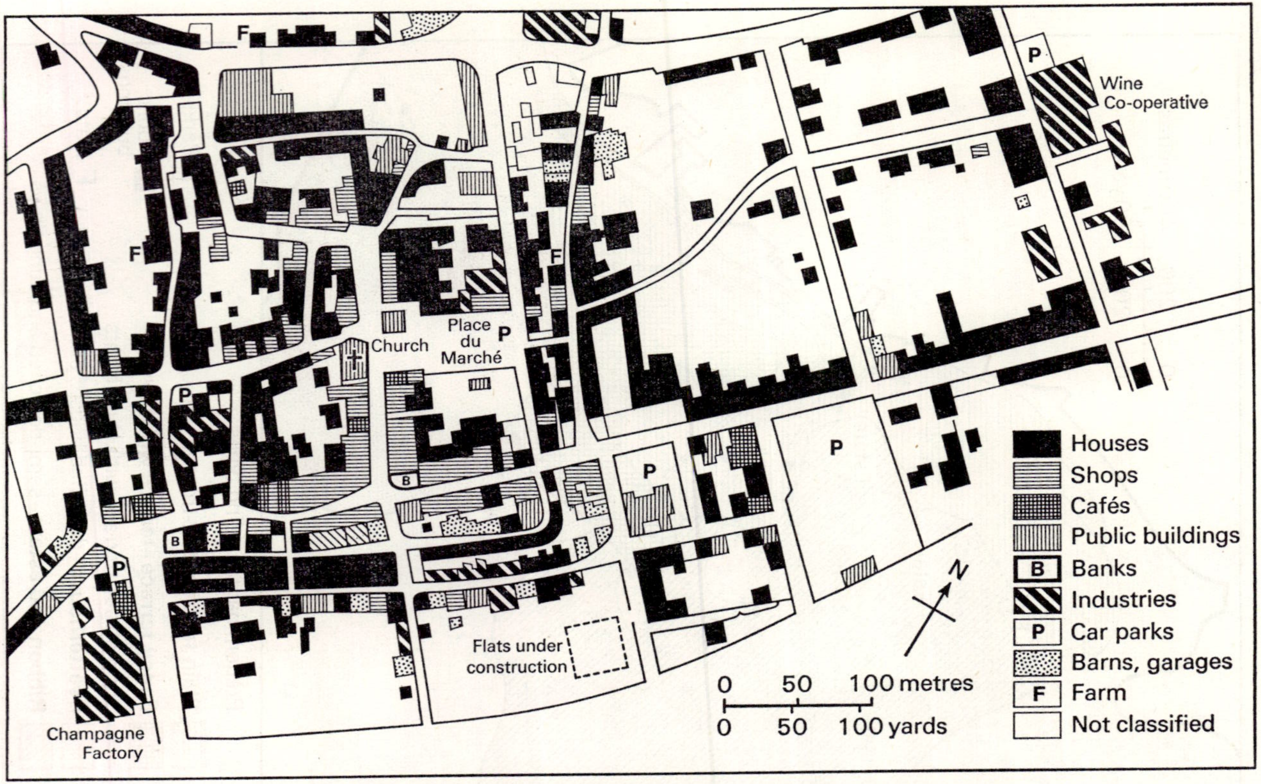

Figure 28 Grevenmacher: land use (Based on student survey, 1968)

APPENDIX 3

A weekend course programme

The organisation of such a course will obviously vary according to the circumstances, but it may be useful to consider the following, which is based on a recent Field Week with students at Grevenmacher, a Luxembourg town on the Moselle. The urban fieldwork took only part of the week, but occupied approximately two or two-and-a-half days, according to the length of time spent on individual assignments.

First morning: Reconnaissance

Grevenmacher is a small place of some 3 000 inhabitants and it was therefore possible to take the whole town as a field of study and to investigate it on foot; in a larger town it would be necessary to concentrate on only a part of it, or on one or two sample areas. As no town map was available, an enlargement of the 1:25 000 map was made by epidiascope projection and then duplicated. The students had the task of completing and correcting this and inserting street names; this was a useful exercise and focused attention on street layout and the possible significance of the street names. Even in a general reconnaissance it is advisable to have specific as well as general observation, and attention should be directed to some aspect such as street names, building material, or architectural style. Time was left at the end of the morning for discussion and pooling of information.

First afternoon: Land-use survey

The map was divided into five sections whose sizes depended on the complexity of the area, and each section was allocated to a group of students. Section boundaries were taken as running down the middle of streets. Land use was recorded on sketch-maps made in the field on the basic classification of Residence, Industry, Commerce and Services, with more detailed notes added. For example, the reconnaissance had shown the importance of cafés, and these were specially noted.

First evening: Entry of land use on a base map

See figure 28. If necessary the base map can be cut into the appropriate sections for this and then re-assembled. Discussion of findings and of proposed individual assignments.

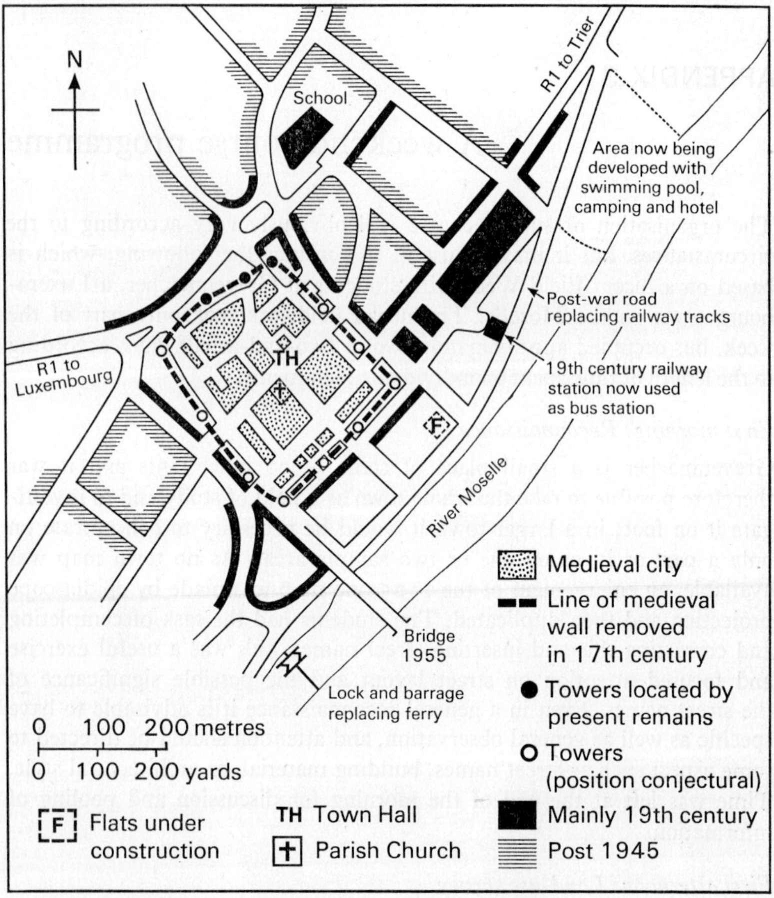

Figure 29 Grevenmacher: growth
(Based on student survey, 1968)

Second day: Work on individual assignments

In the case of Grevenmacher these included studies of:

1) The industries of the town, their nature and location (excluding the wine industry). There were quite a number of these—all small, and mostly carried on in converted dwellings.
2) The wine industry. This was the chief industry and therefore merited separate study.
3) The growth of Grevenmacher, especially the marked effect of the medieval fortifications on the town pattern (*see figure 29*). These fortifications were dismantled in the seventeenth century but some remnants are still visible.
4) The Moselle (recently canalised), its use and its effect on the town.
5) Urban transects from north to south and east to west (two assignments).
6) A detailed study of the location and types of shops.
7) The origin of goods on display.
8) Provision for tourism.
9) Building materials and architectural styles.

Note: Traffic was not studied as it was most remarkable for its absence.

APPENDIX 4

A home-made clinometer

Make a semi-circular protractor in card, marked off and numbered every five degrees as shown.

Glue the paper protractor to a piece of three-ply or hardboard, which may be rectangular or cut to a semi-circle. It is best to cover the whole with an adhesive film such as Fablon.

Fasten a strip of wood behind the upper edge and add a backsight and a foresight. The sights may be two panel pins, or the backsight may be a metal 'V' or a small hole. Alternatively a square wooden tube may be used instead of the wooden strip.

From Point 'A' hang a length of dark, strong thread with a weight on the end. This is a plumb line.

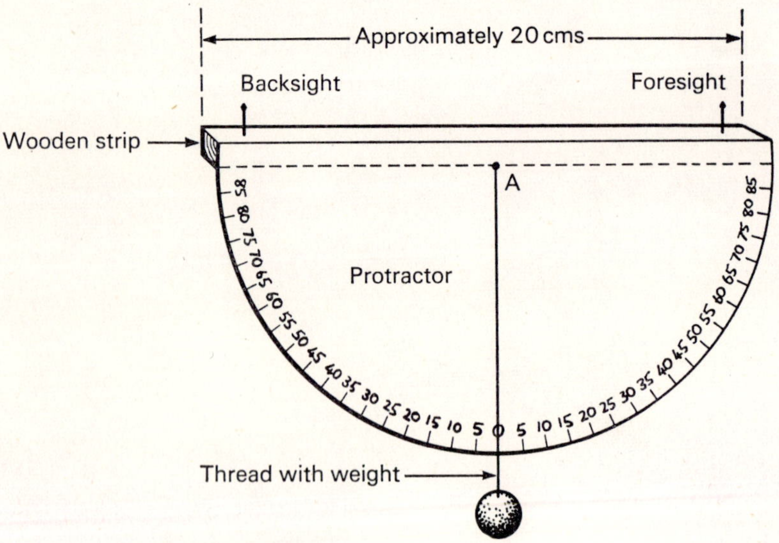

Figure 30

To use the clinometer

The top must be parallel to the slope, with the plumb line hanging freely so that it is vertical. The clinometer must therefore be sighted on to an object (such as a mark on a pole) at the same height above the ground as the observer's eyes. The angle of slope is read from where the plumb line crosses the edge of the protractor. The geometry is as follows:

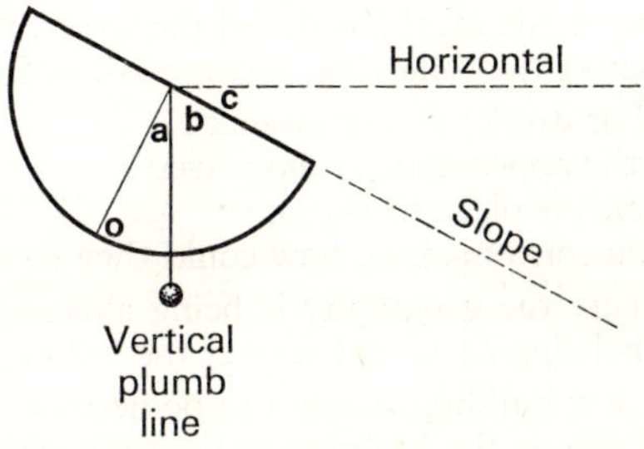

$$\hat{a} + \hat{b} = 90^\circ$$
$$\hat{c} + \hat{b} = 90^\circ$$
$$\therefore \quad \hat{a} = \hat{c} \text{ which is the angle of slope.}$$

Figure 31

Three-dimensional models

This is an effective way of showing spatial distributions—for example, housing density in different parts of a town. A grid is drawn on a base map representing the area. In each square of the grid you then erect a column whose height is proportional to the density of houses in each square. The columns can be made of dowelling and fastened with glue or pushed into pegboard. More fragile models can be made with drinking straws. *Trend surfaces* can be shown by joining the tops of adjacent columns with strips of paper, or by building up the model with clay.

A second distribution can be shown on the same model (for example, number of shops with number of dwellings) by adding a second set of columns distinguished by a different colour, but more than this is liable to be confusing and, of course, trend surfaces cannot be shown.

APPENDIX 5

Basic urban study exercises

1. Write a brief general account of the appearance of the street you live in, paying attention to such things as the kind of buildings, the materials they are made of, the width of the street, and the amount of traffic. Then answer the following, giving reasons for your answers:
   (*a*) Do you like or dislike its appearance?
   (*b*) How could the appearance be improved?
   (*c*) Is it a convenient place to live in?
   (*d*) If there are inconveniences, how could they be remedied?
2. Find a place where the geography is being altered by new building. Describe what is being done and answer the following:
   (*a*) Why is the new building thought to be necessary?
   (*b*) In your opinion, is the building in the right place?
   (*c*) And in the best possible style for the place?
3. If there have been some arguments about a local planning proposal, find out all you can about it—for example, consult the local newspapers, including the letters to the Editor—and summarise the arguments for and against. Give your own opinion.

Source material

4. Get a 1 : 10 000 or 1 : 2 500 map of your area and find your house. (This may not be easy, but you can work it out if you start from a well-known landmark.) Take the map to a part you do know well. Establish where you are on the map and then use the map to get to another point a mile away. Enlarge a section of the map and put in the street names.
5. Find the oldest map of the town that your library has available. Trace the street pattern. On the tracing, draw in red any new streets or alterations to old streets.
6. If one does not exist, make a list of the old maps of the town available in the library.
7. Look at the latest copy of your local newspaper and make notes of any information it gives about the geography of the town—including such things as photographs, house sales and advertisements. Now find the oldest local newspaper available and make similar notes. Compare the two.

Recording

8. Design a recording sheet and code to be used for recording some common, but variable, feature in your street, such as size of front gardens, shapes of television aerials, type of fencing, etc. Use it to collect information and make a distribution map. Note any difficulties.

9. Make a sketch of the front of your house and annotate it suitably; then do the same for the back.
10. Make a measured plan of the ground floor of your house.
11. Draw a front view (elevation) of part of a shopping street and annotate it to show uses of each storey.

Relief and aspect

12. Find out which compass direction the front of your house faces. Observe the movement of the shadows round your house and map them for different times of the day. Which room gets the most sun? Which the least? Explain the effects of aspect on your house and garden.
13. On a 1 : 10 560 or 1 : 10 000 map find the nearest contours and spot heights to your house. What is the altitude (height above Mean Sea Level) of your house? In which direction would you go to (*a*) get higher, (*b*) get lower, (*c*) stay at the same level? Check this in the field. Why may this not agree with the map answer?
14. Find a street with a considerable slope. How has building been influenced by the slope? Illustrate with sketches and diagrams. Try to find another sloping street where the effect has been different, and compare the two.

Geology

15. What is the soil like in your garden? (Colour, depth, texture, water-holding properties, acidity, etc.) Can you find other gardens where the soil is different? Consult a geological map and see if there is any coincidence between soil and rock differences.
16. Find, on a geological map of the town, where there is a change from one rock to another. Visit the place and see if there is any apparent difference, such as a change in slope or soil colour.
17. Find a place where the rock is exposed, as in a cutting or excavation. Describe the rock with the aid of diagrams and photographs, paying particular attention to how it lies in its bed, the thickness of the beds and the angle and direction in which they dip.
18. Look around for an area where buildings are being affected by weathering. Describe the effects and draw sketches and/or take photographs. Compare weathering effects on different materials and on different faces of the same building.

Rivers and water supply

19. Look for any street names which may be connected with water (Brook, Canal, Bridge, Mill, etc.) and see if you can relate them to local streams. Look on old maps for any streams which may be covered over.
20. Is your local water supply 'hard' or 'soft'? Why?
21. If any areas of your town are subject to flooding, try to find the limits of the floods. Explain the reasons for flooding. It will probably help to consult newspaper accounts and reports of the River Board.

Land use

22. Choose one small area where several different types of land use are near each other. Using a simple classification into Houses/Shops/Offices/Industry/Open Space/Others, make a sketch map of the area to show ground-floor land use.

In what ways is this simple classification unsatisfactory? Design another one more suited to the particular area.

Shopping survey

23. Choose a shopping street, or a section of it, and make a sketch map to show what the shops sell. Then answer the following:
  (*a*) Are the goods meant mostly for people who live nearby or for those who come from further away? Or is there a mixture of both?
  (*b*) Are there several shops selling the same sort of thing?
  (*c*) If so, why do you think there is more than one?
  (*d*) Are there any shops selling very expensive articles? If not, why not? Or if so, why so?
  (*e*) Is it a convenient place for shopping? (Easy to get to, easy to cross the street, easy for parking, on a bus route, etc.)
  (*f*) Is there any difference between the shops on one side of the street and those on the other? If so, why?
  (*g*) How many belong to a 'chain' of shops (Boots, Woolworths, Burtons, etc.)? If some do, why do you think this street was chosen for them?
  (*h*) Are there any other things (cafés, banks, etc.) which are of use to the shoppers?

Industry

24. Using a classified telephone directory or a town directory and a street map, plot the positions of the biggest number of factories producing one kind of thing. Try to explain why they are distributed in that particular way.
25. Choose a local factory. Observe it and note its position and its shape; the numbers of workers who leave, and how large a proportion are women (you cannot *count* them, of course, but you can get an idea of whether there is a big labour force or not); the number and type of lorries that come and go, and what they carry; how much storage space there is, and where it is. You can learn quite a lot by just looking, but, of course, it is better to arrange a visit if possible.
26. Are there any unused factories? If so, plot them on a map and try to find out why they went out of business. Has this any relation to their geographical position?
27. If there is an industrial estate in or by the town, find out what the different factories make. Why do they make those sorts of things?

Townscape

28. Describe the townscape of the street in which you live. Select *four* features which you think are distinctive characteristics of this townscape. Select another street which looks different from yours. Describe the differences. Select four visual features of this second street which help to make it appear different from your own.
29. Choose a residential street in (*a*) an old part of the town (*b*) a new part. Describe the differences in appearance between the two. Which would you prefer to live in, and why?

Transport

30. At fixed intervals during a day, count the number of cars parked in your street. When are the maximum and minimum densities? Attempt to explain this. If you take the registration numbers of the cars you can also note their length of stay.
31. Count the number of people at your nearest bus stop at intervals during (*a*) a week-day, (*b*) a Saturday. Show these numbers on a graph or diagram and attempt to explain the variations it shows. Ideally, observations should be made for each bus departure, but if this cannot be done you should arrange your observations to cover maximum and minimum usage (something like early morning, mid-morning, mid-day, early and late afternoon, early and late evening).
32. Trace from a map of your town, or of the main shopping and business area, all parts used by road vehicles (roads, car parks, garages, delivery yards for shops, bus depots). By putting the tracing over graph paper and counting squares, calculate the percentage of land used by road vehicles.

Urban growth

33. On a map of your town mark the areas which have been built since 1918. This will be easy if you can find the appropriate map for the time, but can be done reasonably accurately by observing building styles. All Council building will belong to this period. Some of the building will be in the central part where old buildings have been replaced or spaces filled in, but most will be towards the edges where land was available. If your town is too large for this, do the map for a wedge from the centre outwards.

    Attempt to account for the location of the new building.
34. Draw a graph of the town's population given by the Census returns from 1801. Try to account for any sudden increase in population.
35. From old maps, local histories, personal observation, street names, etc., locate the historic core of your town, show its position on the map, and suggest reasons for its position. Is it still the busiest part of the town? If not, why not?
36. Using the oldest and newest directories available, note the main industries of the town and their location and show them on a map. Account for any changes in type and distribution.

Regions in towns

37. Note the characteristic geographical features of the area immediately around your house. Determine how far these extend before some features start to change. On this basis show on a town map the boundaries of your region and briefly describe its characteristics.
38. Take a bus journey across the town and mark on a map where you appear to pass from one region to another. Give descriptive names to these regions.

Towns in regions

39. Consulting a bus timetable, draw a map of the bus routes out of your town, putting in all the bus stops. At each one put in the number of buses to and from your town which call there on a week-day. Mark the width of the road proportional to the number of buses (e.g. 1mm to 10 buses).
40. Visit the town market and find out where the various products on sale have been sent from. Show this by means of a map.
41. Find out for (*a*) a large store, (*b*) the town's newspaper, the places to which deliveries are made. Show this on a map. Why is the area of delivery not a circle?
42. Map the position of all places which send advertisements to the local paper. Make a classification code which will show on the map what kind and how many products and services are advertised from each place.
43. If the information is available find out for a large factory in your town how many people are employed and how many of these live outside the town. Draw a diagram to show this proportion. If you can find out the numbers who live in the various places around your town, draw a map to show this and suggest why these particular places are chosen.

Classification

44. How would you classify your town on the basis of (*a*) its physical site, (*b*) its main economic function? Give examples and, if possible, statistics to support your view.
45. Study a nearby town to decide whether it is of a higher, lower, or the same rank as your own. Say on what facts you base your decision.